Rock Around The Keyboard

WITH JUST 4 CHORDS

By Pete Dino

Copyright © 1992 Ekay Music, Inc.
223 Katonah Avenue, Katonah, NY 10536

Table of Contents

Abracadabra 7

Baby I'm-A Want You 10

The Beat Goes On 12

Bye Bye Love 14

Chain of Fools 16

Chariots of Fire 20

Come Go With Me 26

Crimson and Clover 28

Crystal Blue Persuasion 23

Dance to the Music 30

Deep in the Heart of Texas 34

Games People Play 36

A Groovy Kind of Love 38

Higher and Higher 40

A Horse With No Name 42

I Saw Her Standing There 44

I Think We're Alone Now 46

If You Love Me (Let Me Know) 48

Itsy Bitsy Teenie Weenie Yellow Polkadot Bikini 52

Jailhouse Rock 54

Kansas City 56

La Bamba 58

Land of a Thousand Dances 60

Lean On Me 62

Love Me 64

Title	Page
Love Potion No. 9	66
Mack the Knife	33
Make It With You	68
Me and You and a Dog Named Boo	70
Moments to Remember	72
Mony Mony	74
My Boy Lollipop	76
Oh, Oh, I'm Falling in Love Again	78
Oh Carol	80
Party Doll	82
Put a Little Love in Your Heart	84
Rock Around the Clock	86
The Rose	90
Roses Are Red (My Love)	92
Short Shorts	94
Shout	96
Stand By Me	98
Summertime Blues	87
Theme from A Summer Place	100
Turn, Turn, Turn	103
Wake Up, Little Susie	106
When a Man Loves a Woman	109
Yellow Rose of Texas	112
You Belong to the City	114
You Were On My Mind	118

A Note About The Chord Symbols Used In This Book

Slash chords, such as C/E, are used from time to time in these arrangements. They indicate the name of the chord (in this case, C Major), and the tone to be played in the bass (in this case, the note E).

One other special feature of the chord symbols is the occasional use of parentheses to indicate optional tones. In the symbol C (maj 7), for instance, the chord is C, but the major seventh may be added for a fuller or more colorful sound.

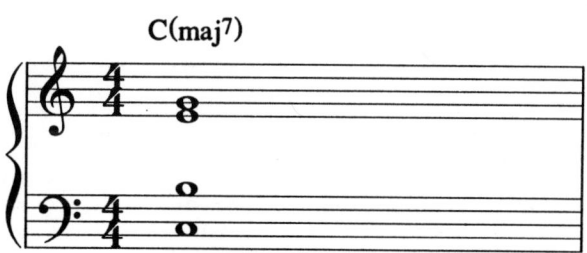

Abracadabra

Words and Music by
STEVE MILLER

The Beat Goes On

Words and Music by
SONNY BONO

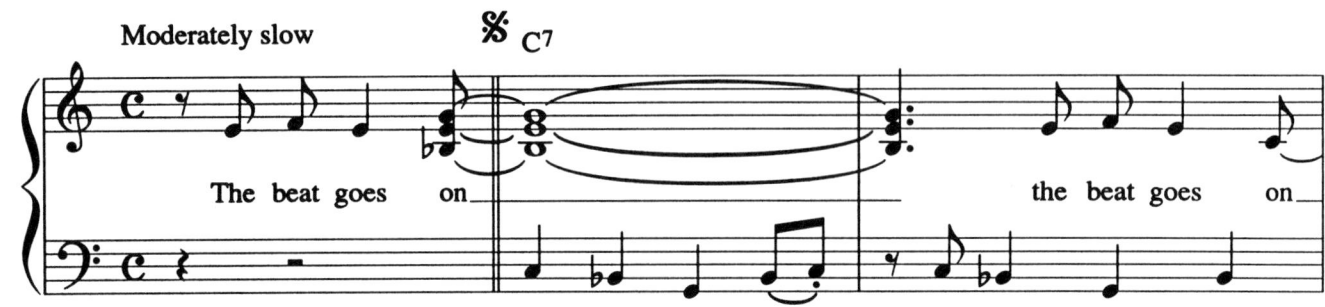

Copyright © 1967 Cotillion Music, Inc. & Chris-Marc Music
All Rights Administered by Warner-Tamerlane Publishing Corp.
All Rights Reserved   Used by Permission

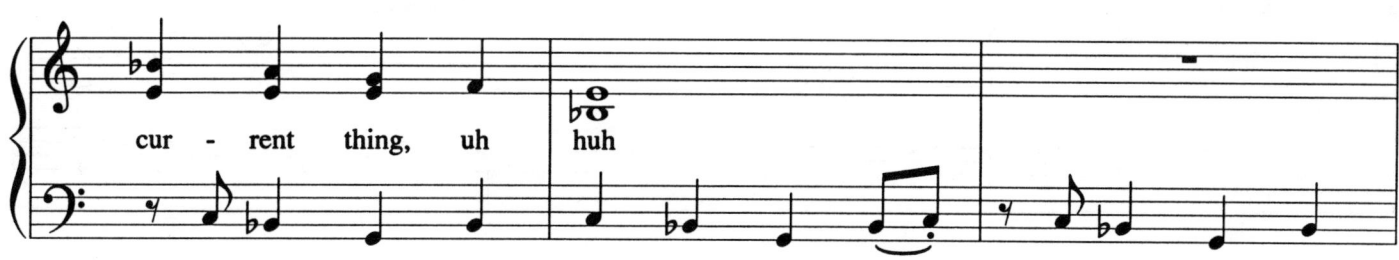

Chain of Fools

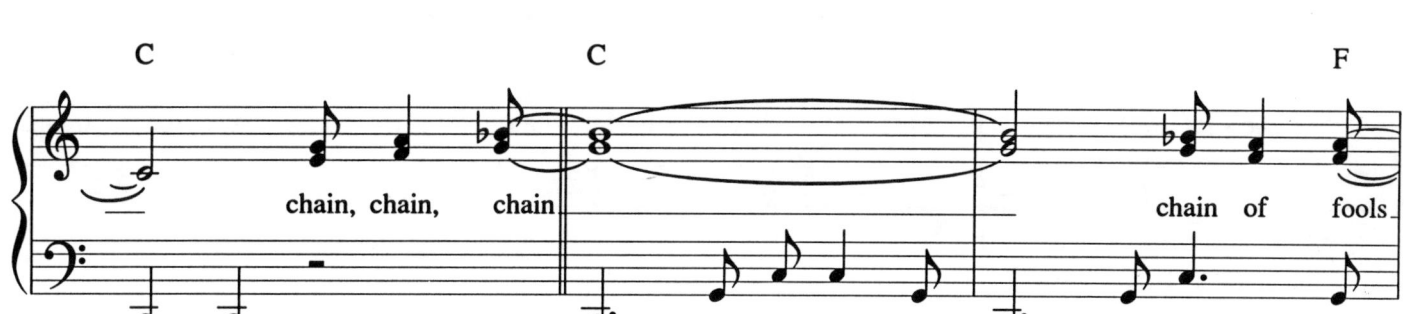

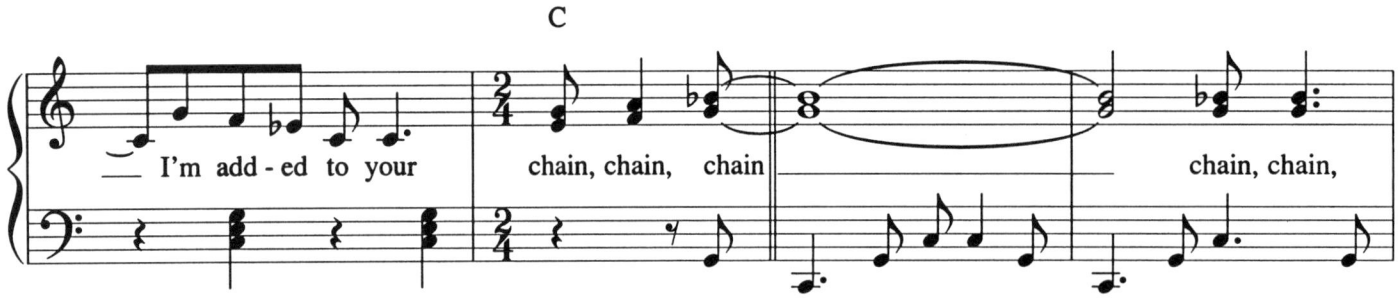

Chariots of Fire

Composed by
VANGELIS

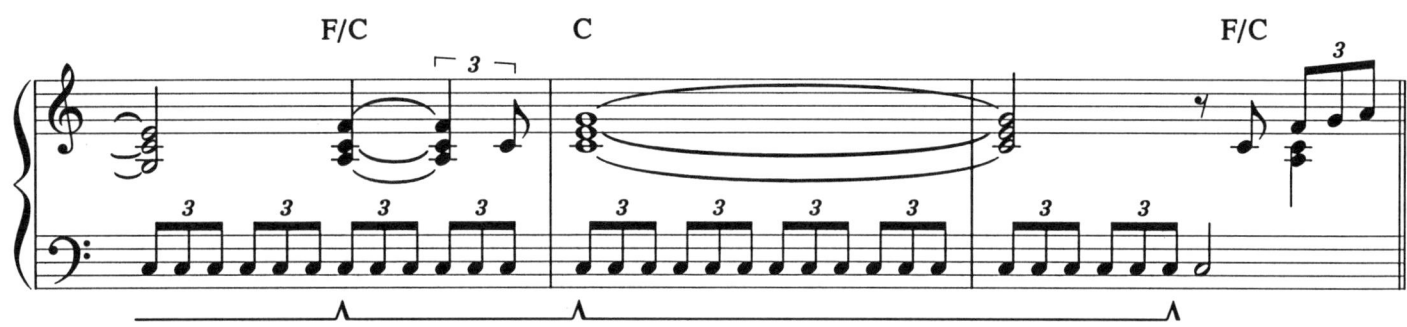
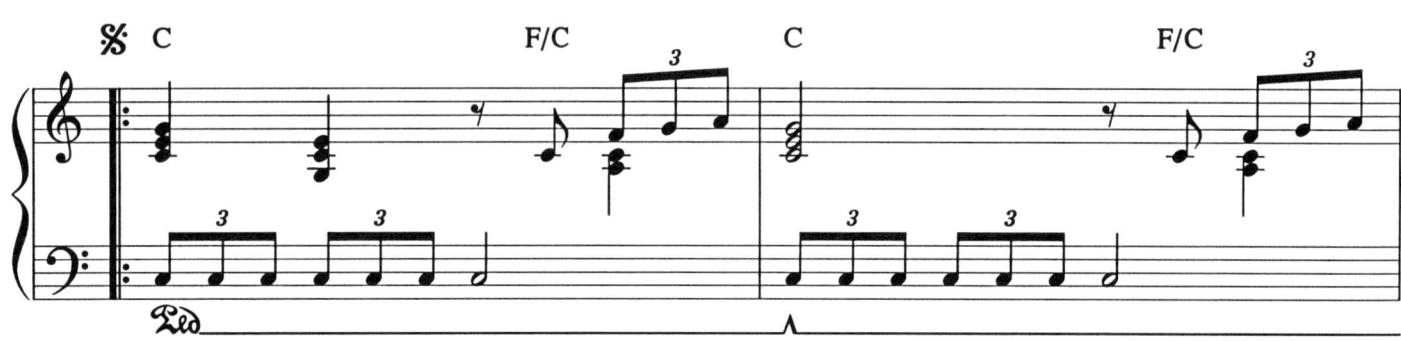
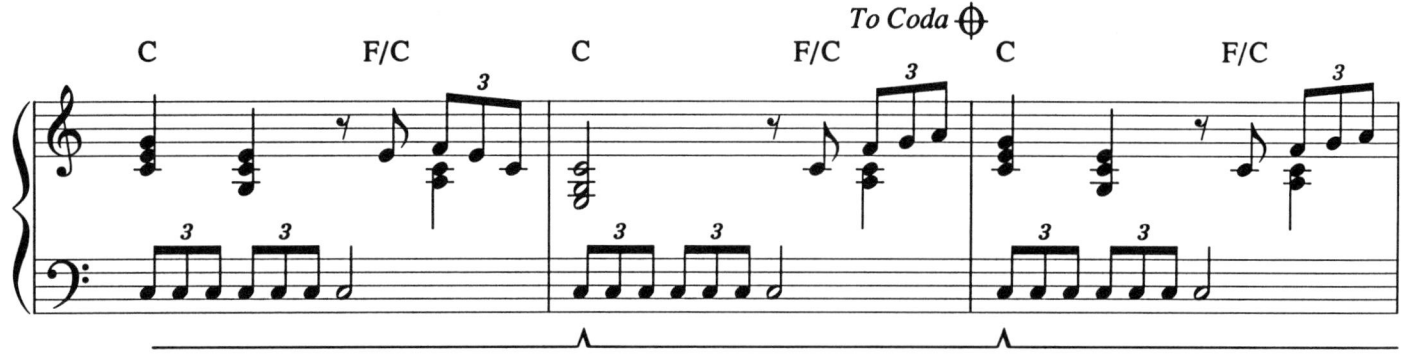

Copyright © 1981 SPERIC B.V.
All Rights for the World, except Holland, Administered by WB MUSIC CORP.
All Rights Reserved   Used by Permission

Crystal Blue Persuasion

Words and Music by
TOMMY JAMES, MIKE VALE and ED GRAY

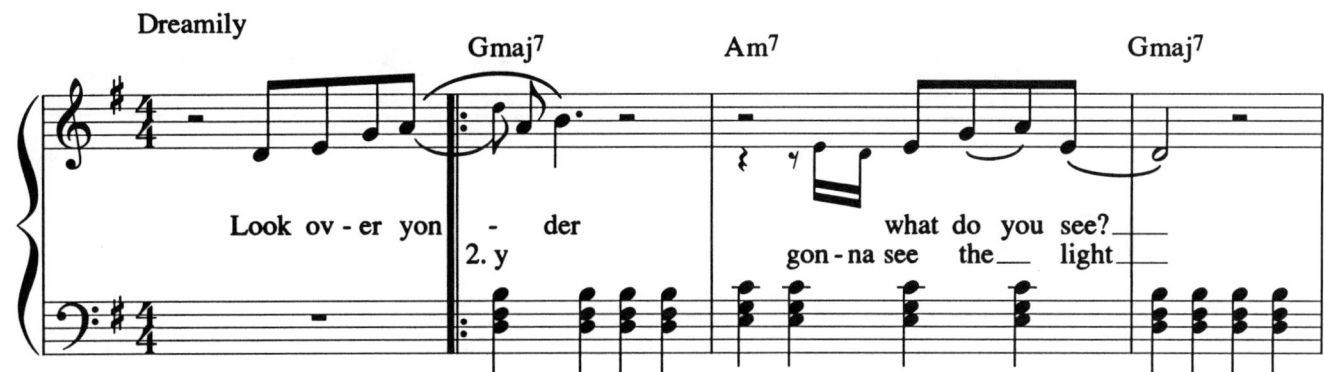
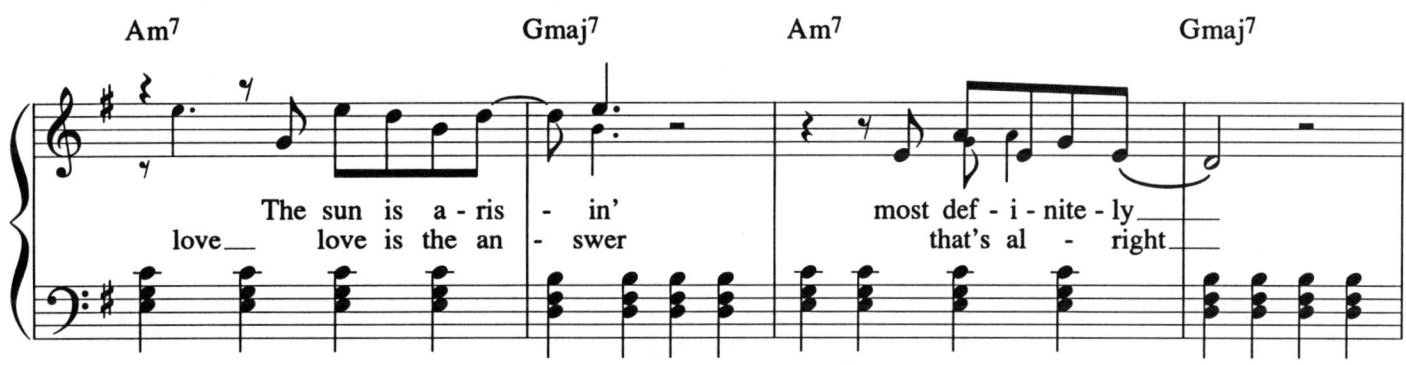

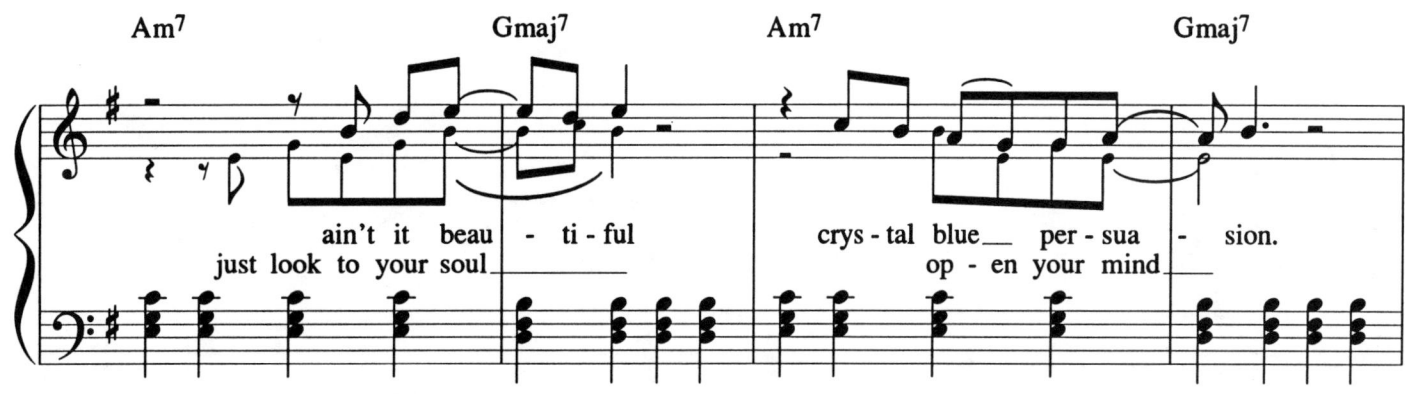

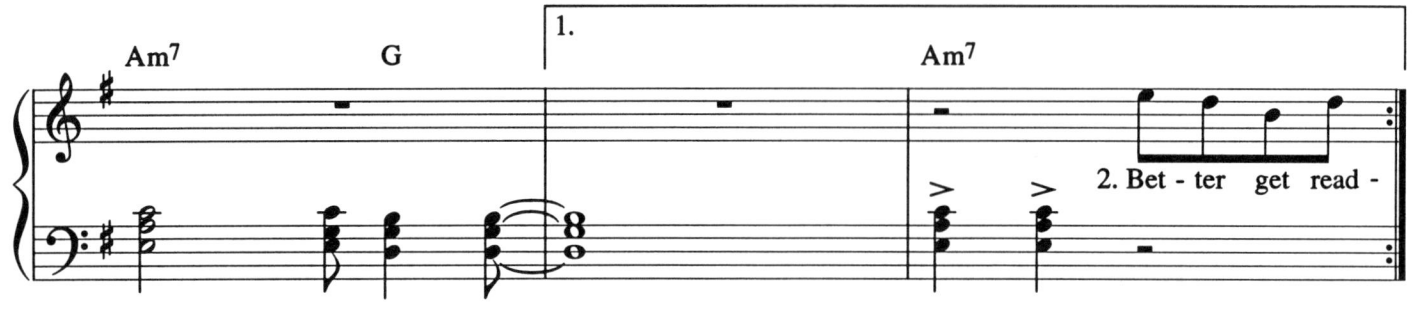
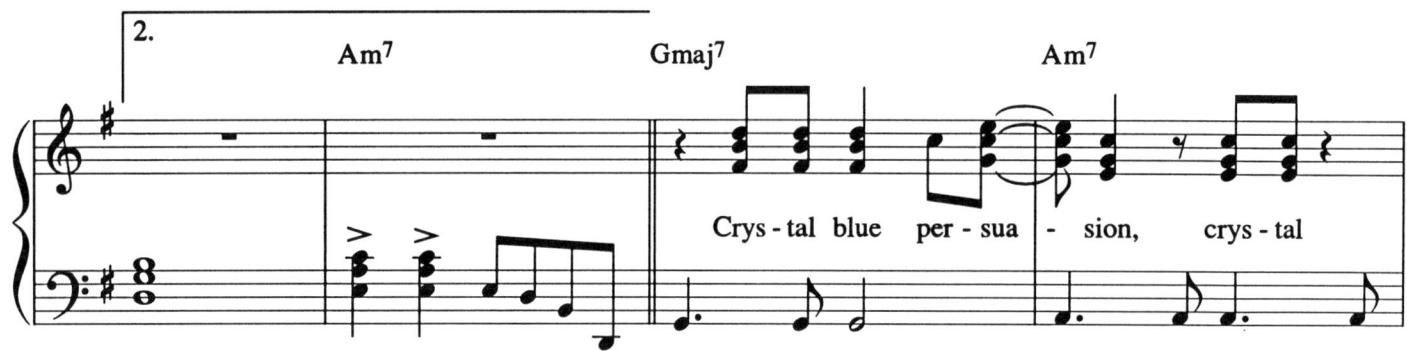

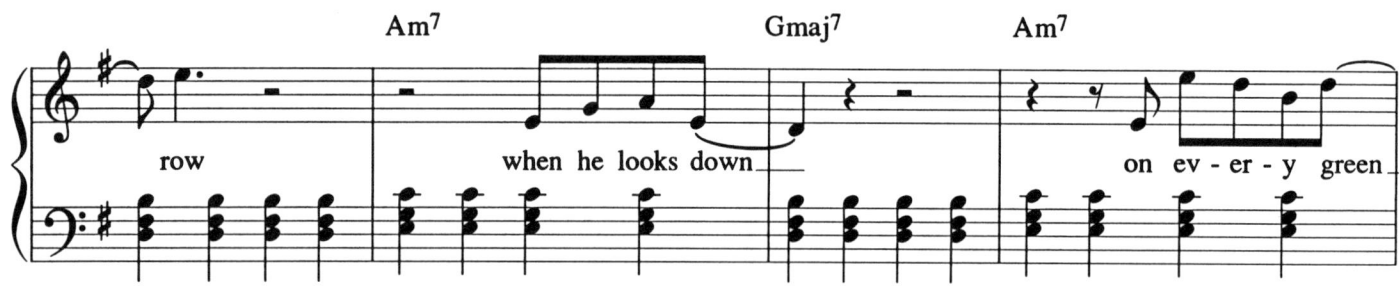

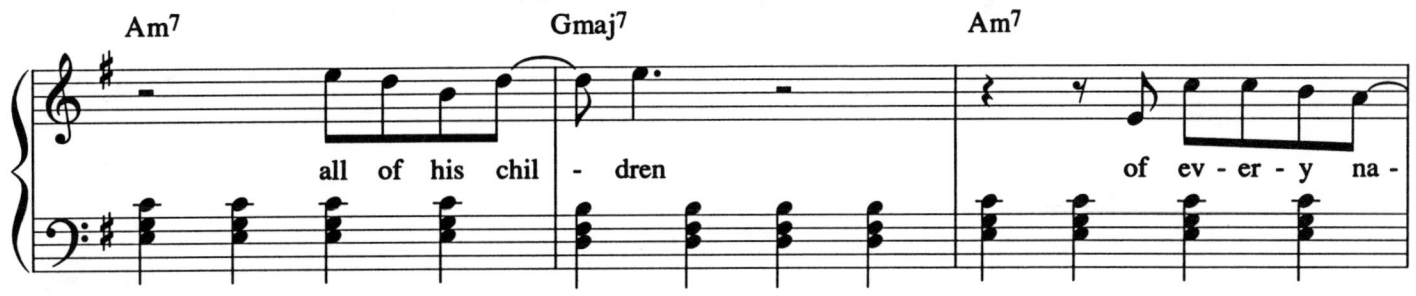

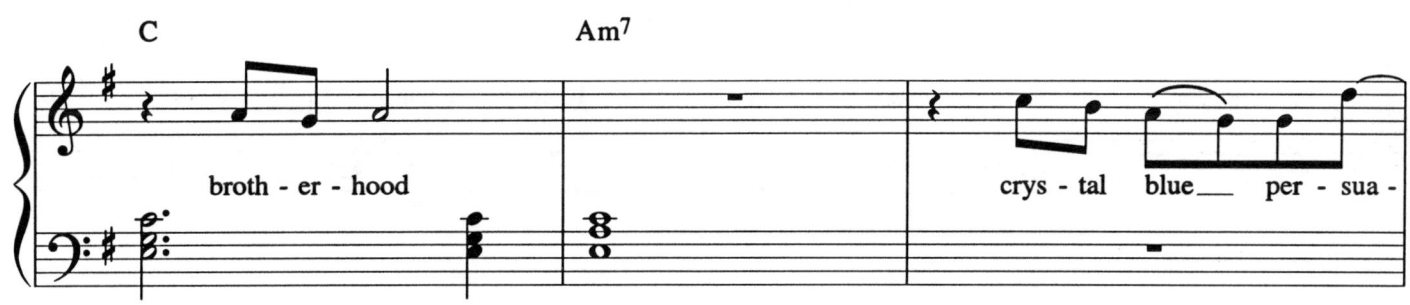
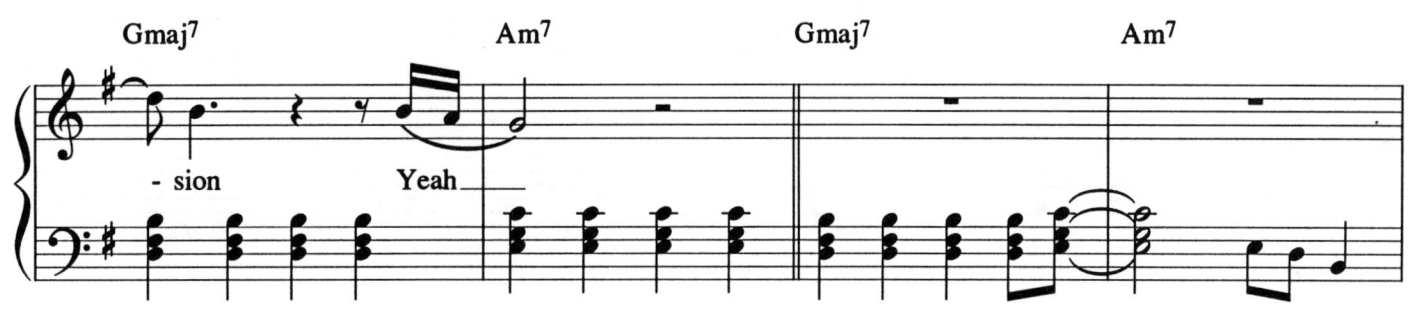
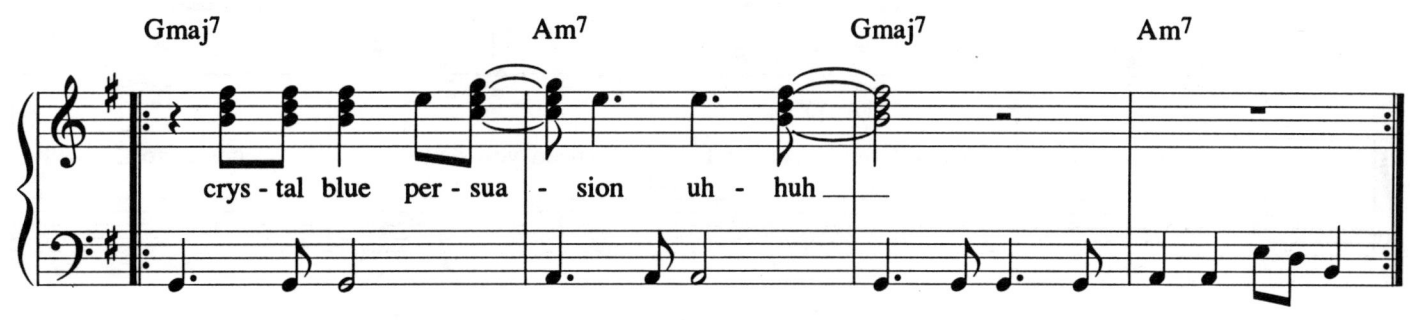

Come Go With Me

By C.E. QUICK

Crimson and Clover

Words and Music by
PETER LUCIA and
TOMMY JAMES

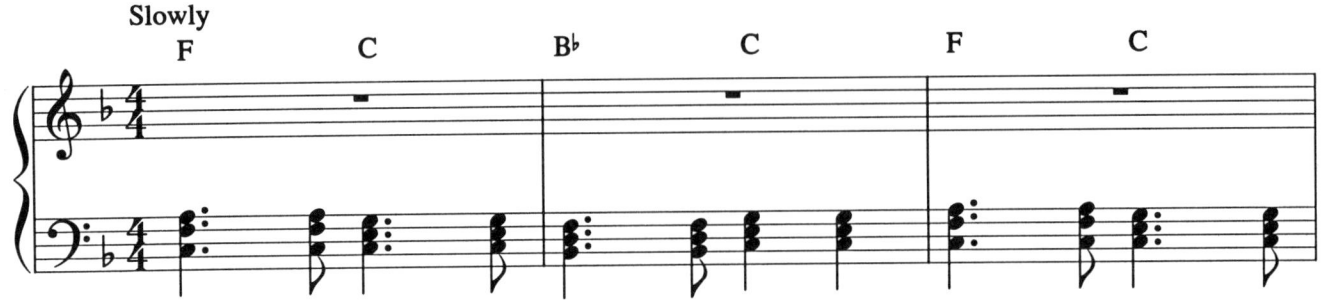
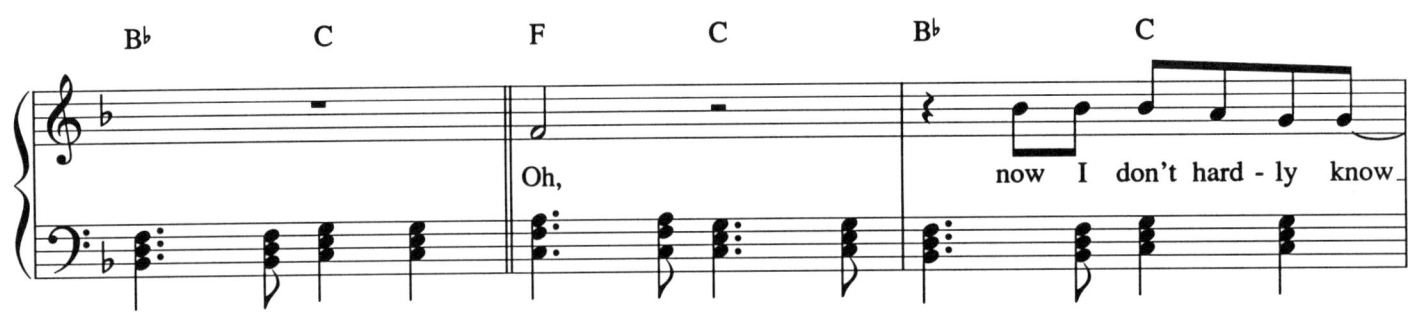

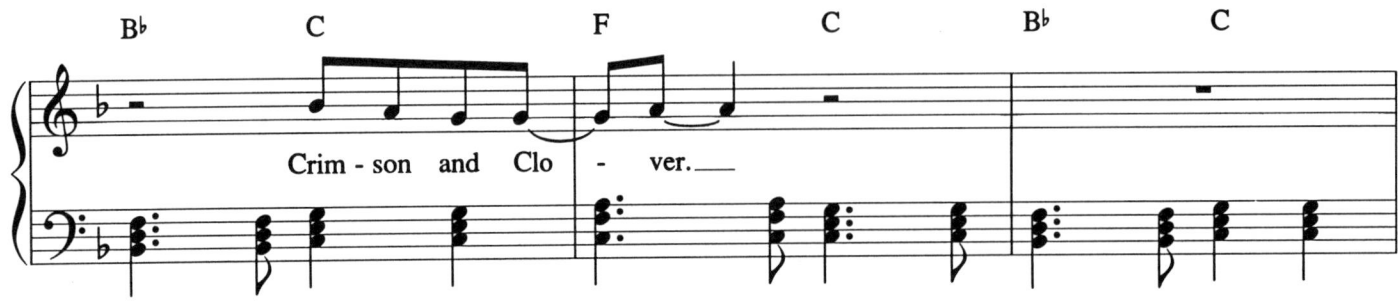

Dance to the Music

Words and Music by
SYLVESTER STEWART

Copyright © 1968 MIJAC MUSIC
All Rights Administered by WARNER-TAMERLANE PUBLISHING CORP.
All Rights Reserved Used by Permission

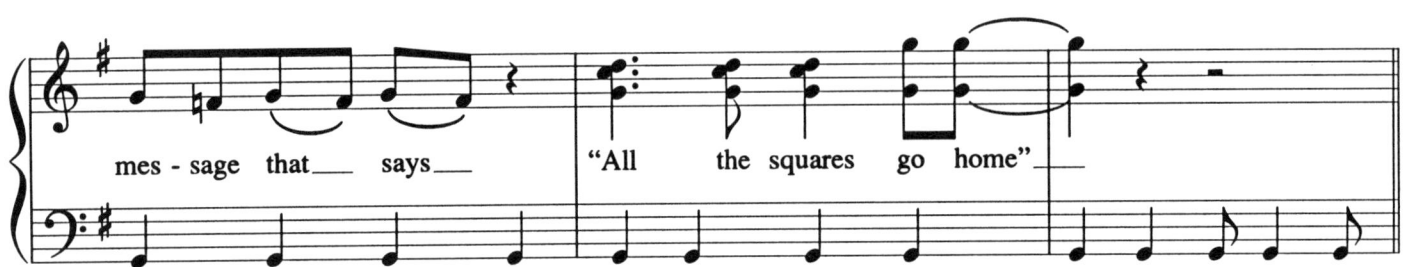
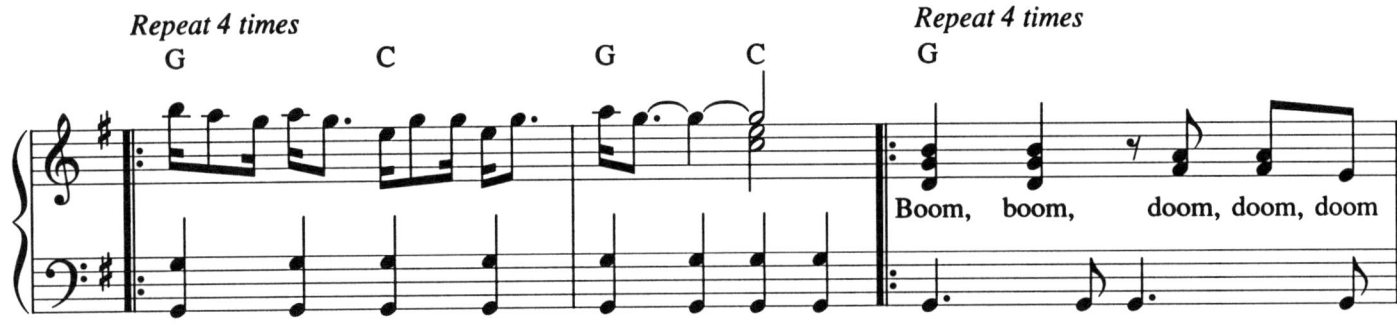
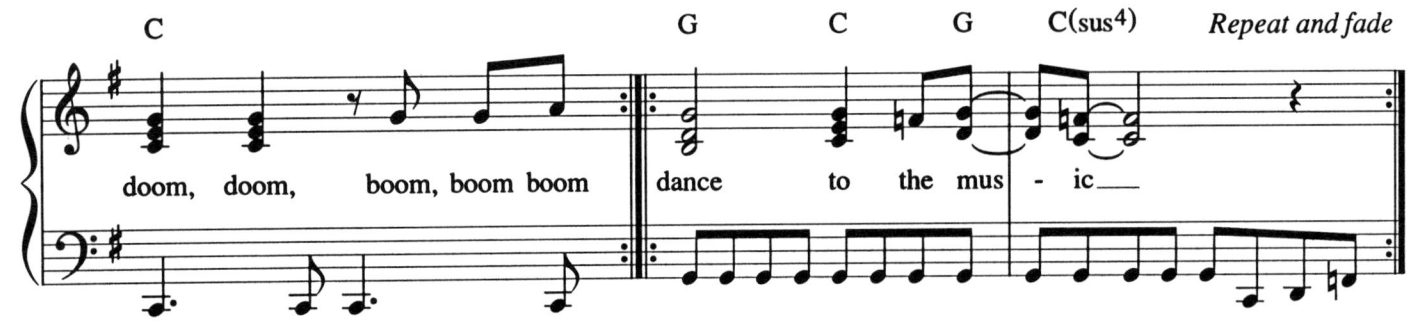

Mack the Knife

Original German Words by BERT BRECHT
English Words by MARC BLITZSTEIN
Music by KURT WEILL

Deep in the Heart of Texas

By JUNE HERSHEY
and DON SWANDER

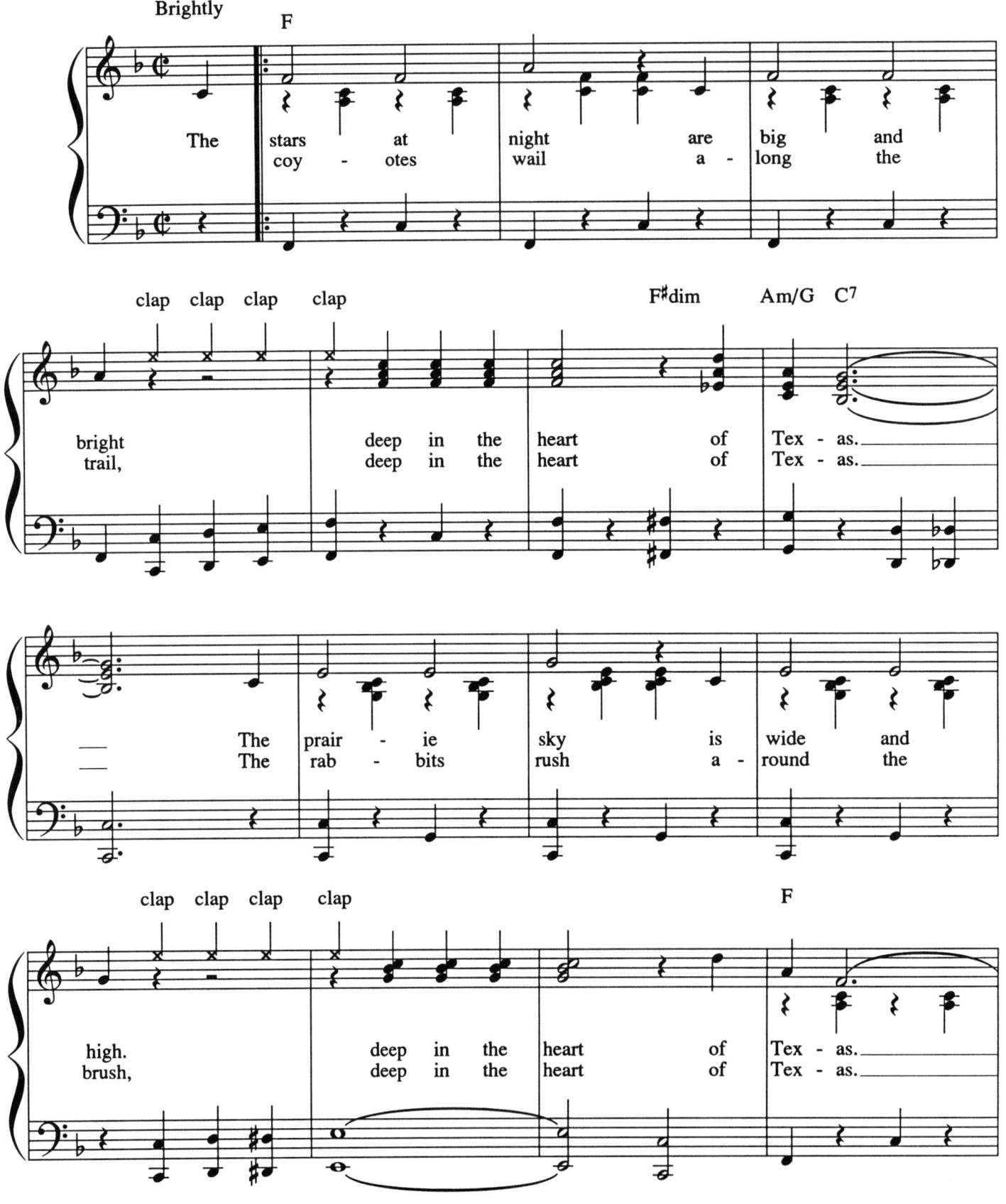

34

Games People Play

By JOE SOUTH

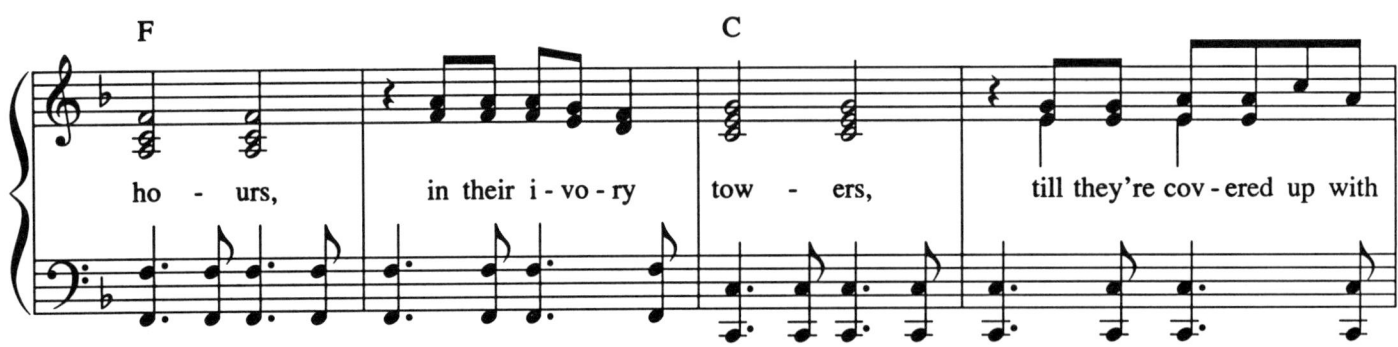

Copyright © 1968, 1970 by LOWERY MUSIC CO., INC., P.O. Box 9687, Atlanta, GA 30319
International Copyright Secured   Made in U.S.A.   All Rights Reserved   Used by Permission

37

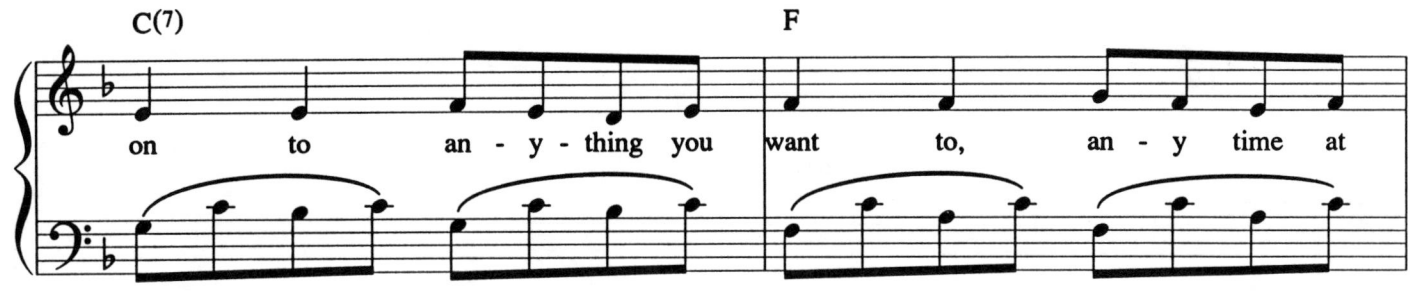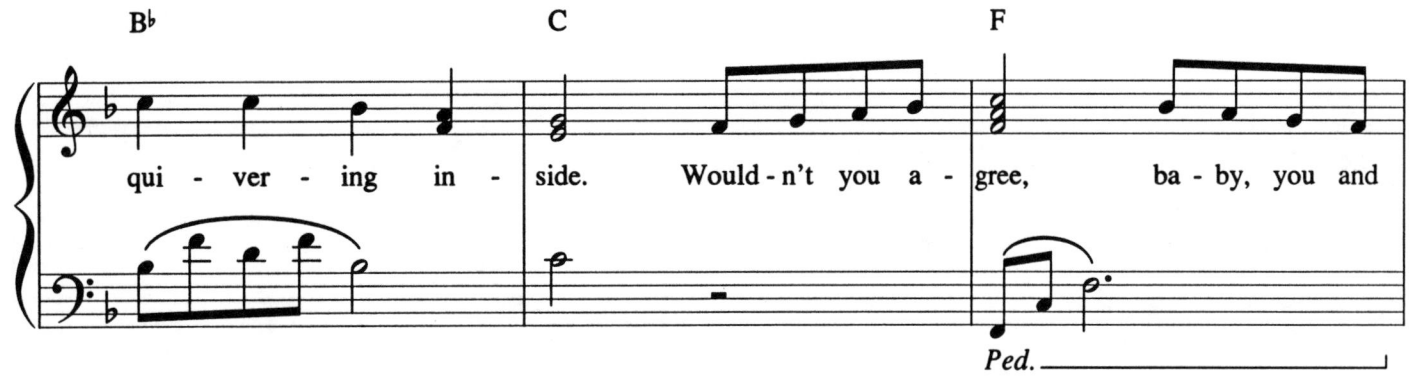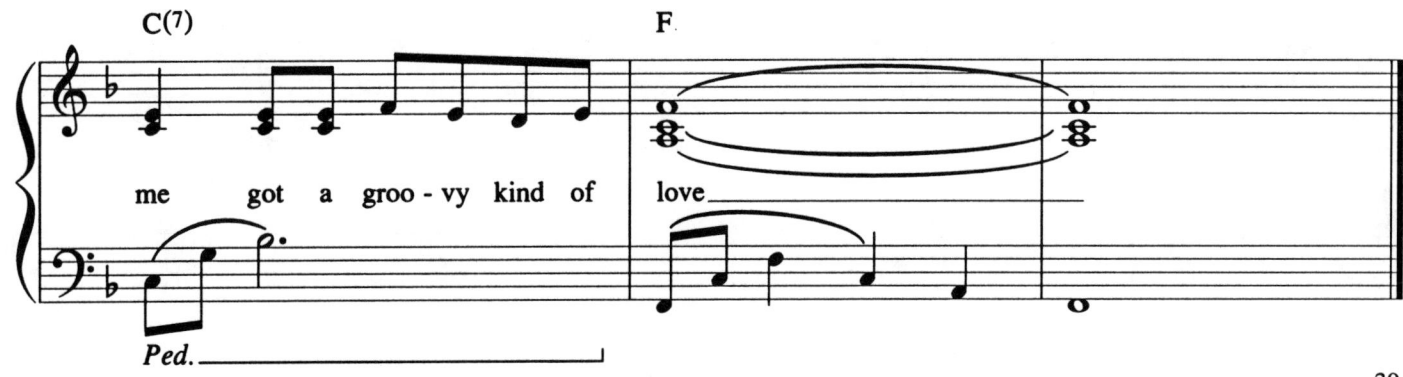

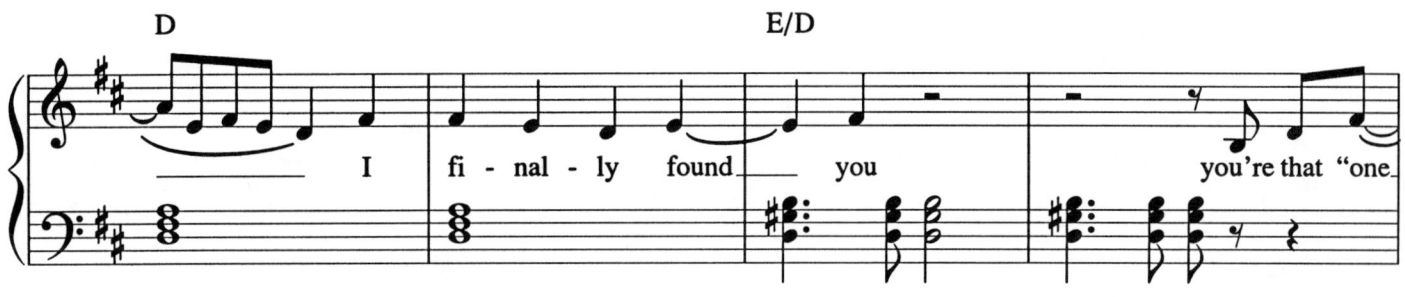
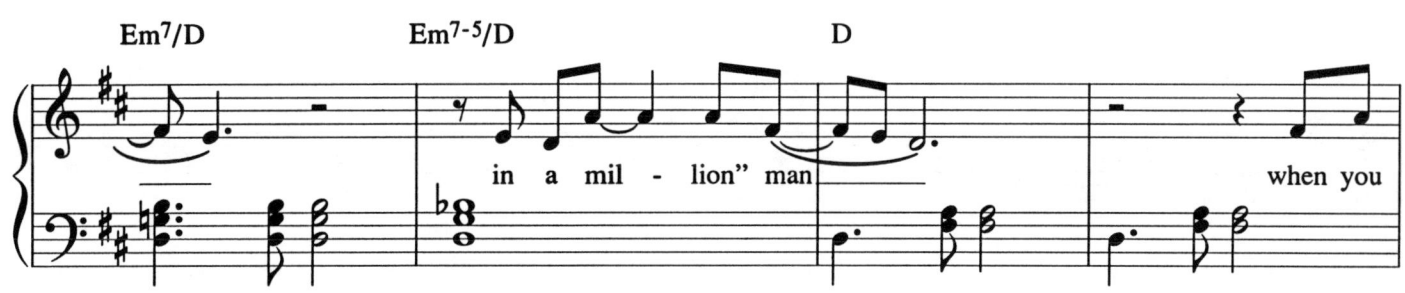
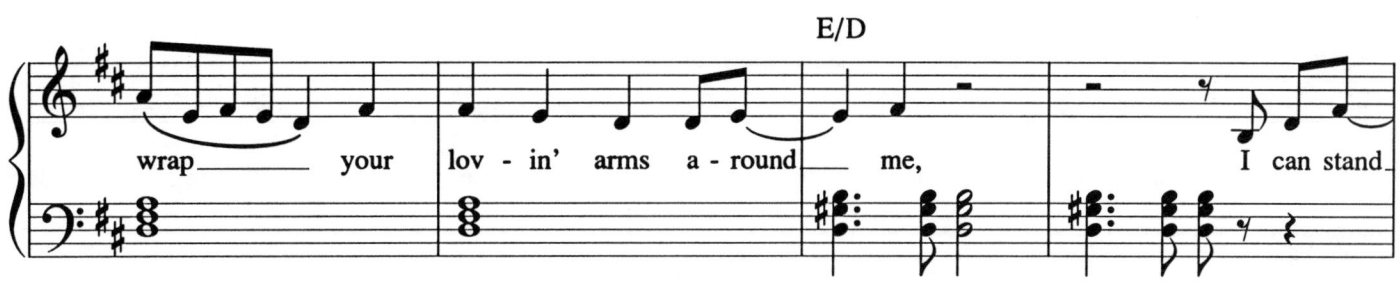
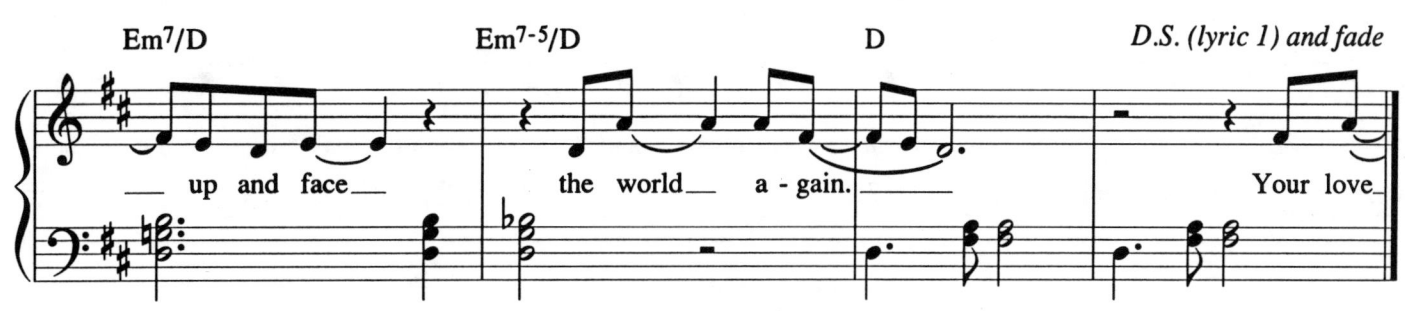

A Horse With No Name

Words and Music by
DEWEY BUNNELL

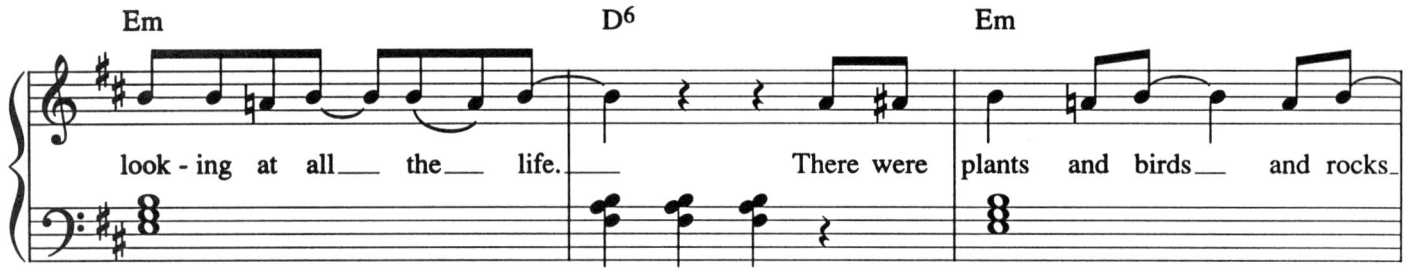
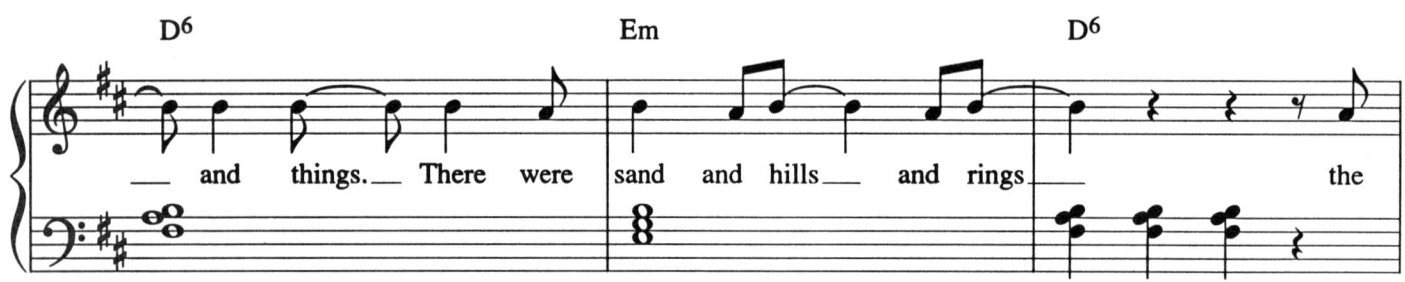

Copyright © 1971 WARNER BROS. MUSIC LIMITED
All Rights for the Western Hemisphere controlled by WB MUSIC CORP.
All Rights Reserved   Used by Permission

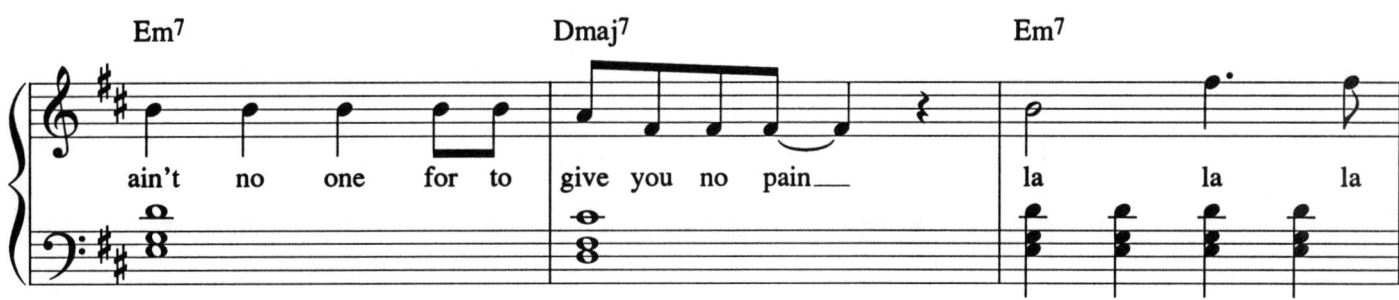
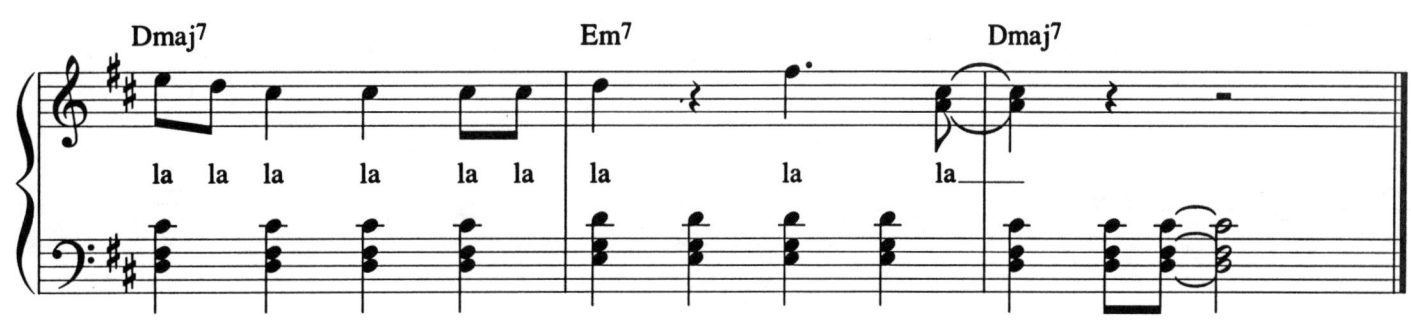

I Think We're Alone Now

Words and Music by
RITCHIE CORDELL

46

Itsy Bitsy Teenie Weenie Yellow Polkadot Bikini

Words and Music by
PAUL J. VANCE
and LEE POCKRISS

Moderately
Chorus:

She was a- | fraid to come out of the | lock - er. She was as
fraid to come out in the | o - pen, And so a
fraid to come out of the | wa - ter, And I

ner - vous as she could | be. She was a- | fraid to come out of the
blan - ket a - round her she | wore; She was a- | fraid to come out in the
won - der what she's gon - na | do; Now she's a- | fraid to come out of the

lock - er. She was a- | fraid that some - bo - dy would | see. } *(Two, three, four,*
o - pen, And so she | sat bun - dled up on the | shore.
wa - ter, And the | poor lit - tle girl's turn - ing | blue.

tell the peo - ple what she wore.) It was an | it - sy bit - sy tee - nie wee - nie

yel - low pol - ka - dot bi - ki - ni | that she wore for the | first time to - day. An

Copyright © 1960 (Renewed) Music Sales Corporation & Emily Music
International Copyright Secured All Rights Reserved Used by Permission

Jailhouse Rock

Words and Music by
JERRY LEIBER and MIKE STOLLER

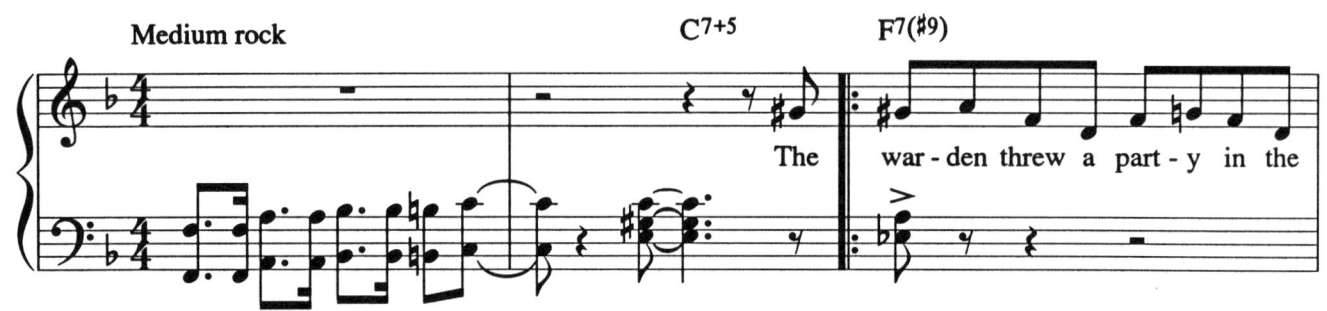

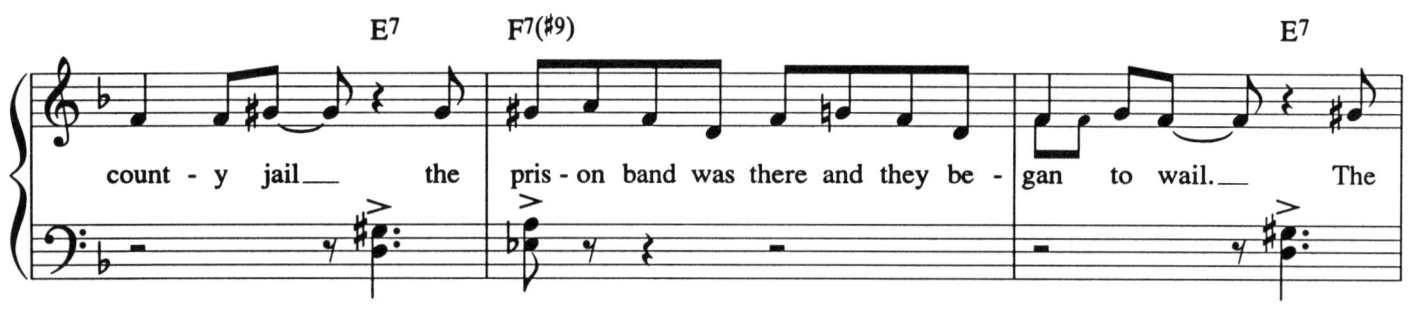

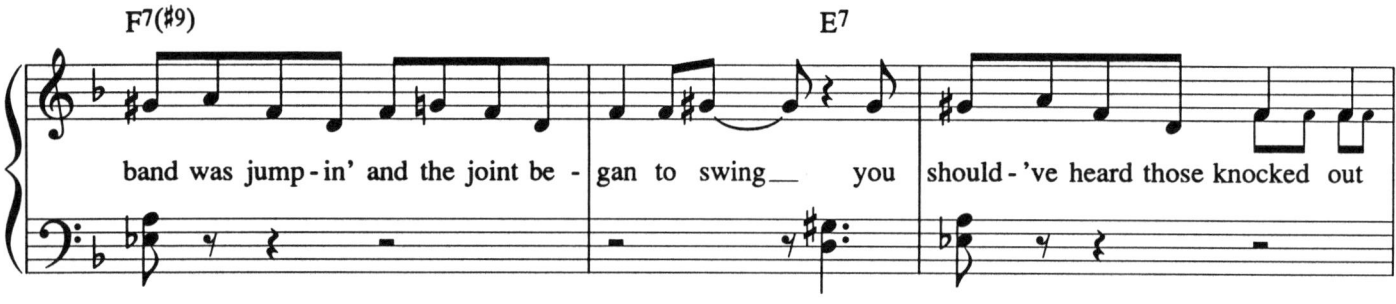

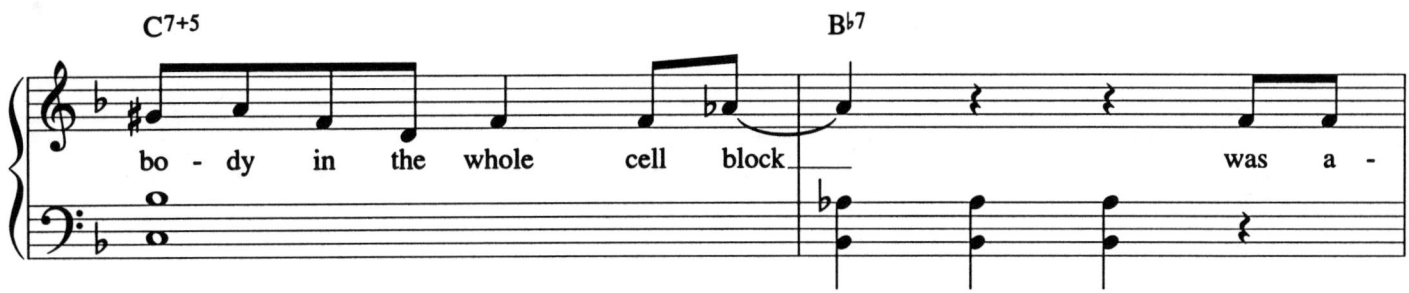

Additional Lyrics

2. Spider Murphy played the tenor saxophone.
   Little Joe was blowin' on the slide trombone.
   The drummer boy from Illinois went crash, boom, bang.
   The whole rhythm section was the purple gang.

3. Number Forty-seven said to Number Three,
   "You're the cutest jailbird I ever did see.
   I sure would be delighted with your company.
   Come on and do the Jailhouse Rock with me."

4. The sad sack was a-sittin' on a block of stone,
   Way over in the corner weeping all alone.
   The warden said, "Hey buddy, don't you be no square.
   If you can't find a partner, use a wooden chair!"

5. Shifty Henry said to Bugs, "For Heaven's sake,
   No one's lookin'; now's our chance to make a break."
   Bugsy turned to Shifty and he said, "Nix, nix;
   I wanna stick around a while and get my kicks!"

Kansas City

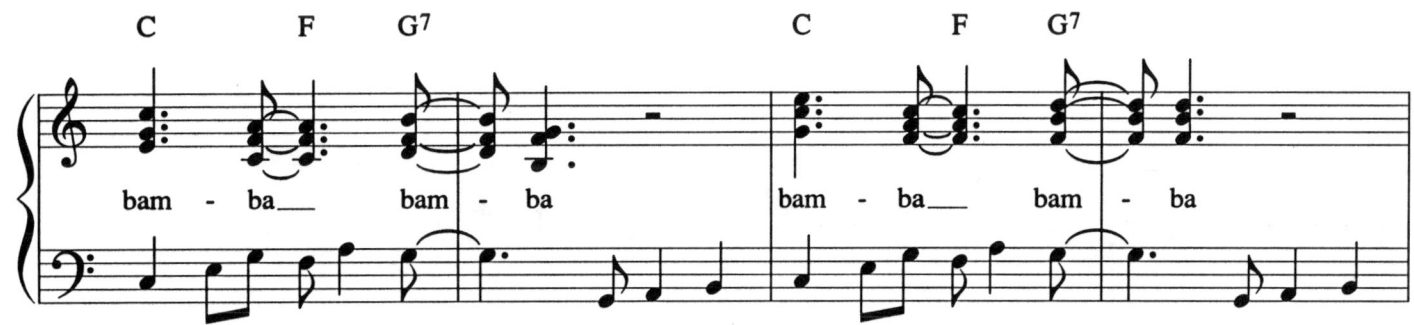
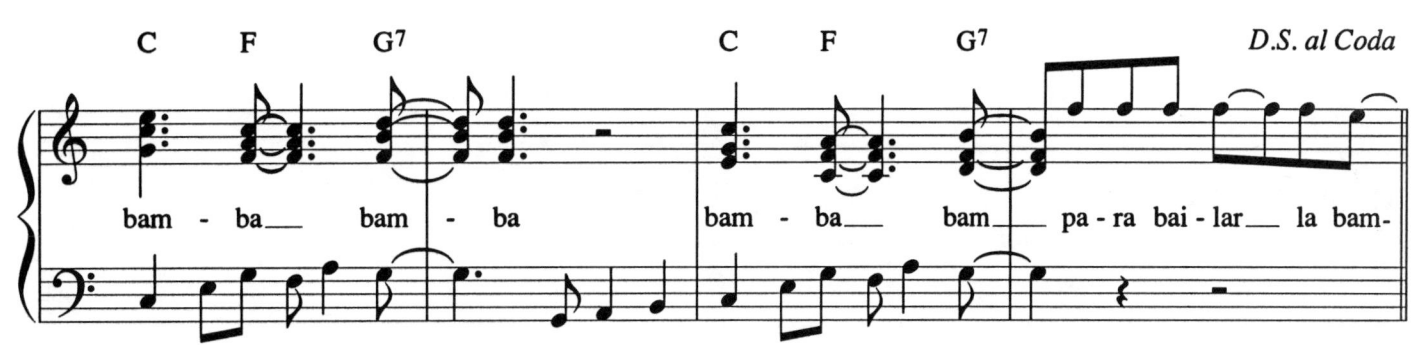
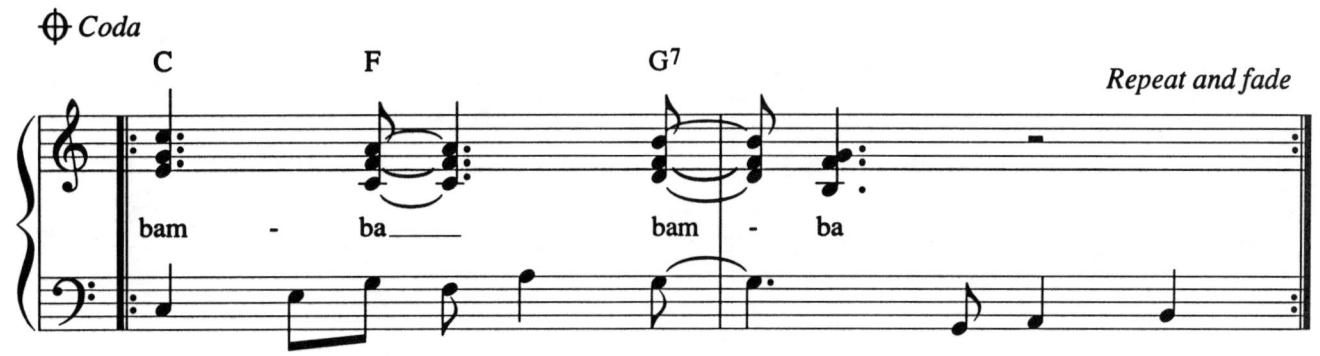

Land of a Thousand Dances

Words and Music by
CHRIS KENNER

Love Potion No. 9

Words and Music by
JERRY LEIBER and MIKE STOLLER

Make It With You

Words and Music by
DAVID GATES

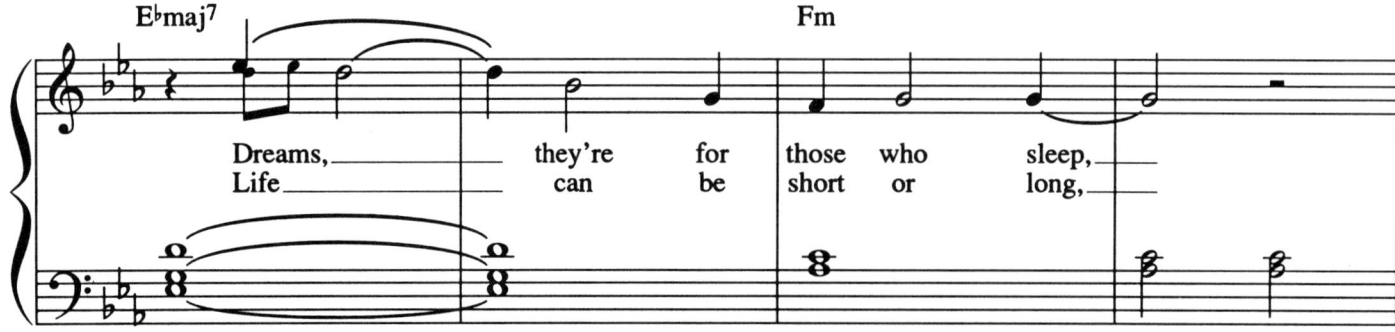

Hey_____ have you ev - er tried_____ real - ly reach - ing out_____ for the oth - er side?
No_____ you don't know me well_____ n'ev - 'ry lit - tle thing_____ on - ly time will tell.

I may be climb - ing on_____ rain - bows_____ but ba - by here goes._____ (Ba - by you know_____ that.)
But you be - lieve - ing the things_____ that I do, And we'll_____ see it through._____

Dreams,_____ they're for those who sleep,_____
Life_____ can be short or long,_____

Copyright © 1970 by Colgem-EMI Music Inc.
All Rights Reserved   Used by Permission

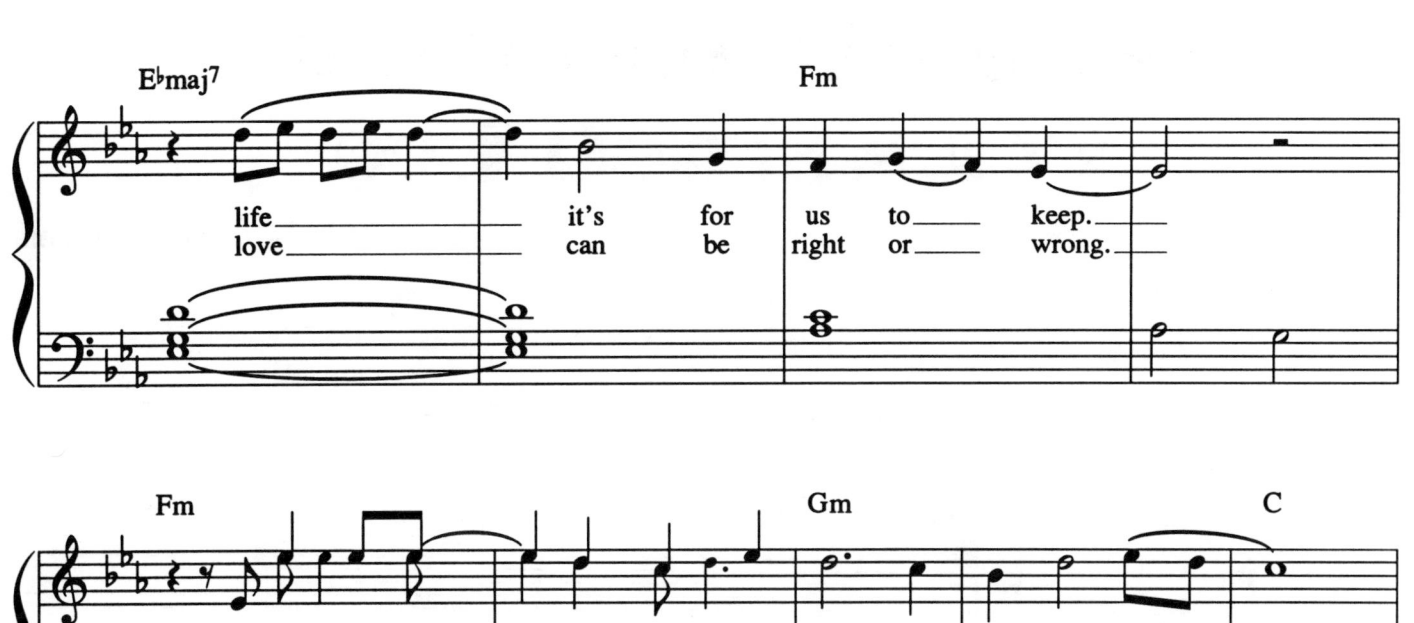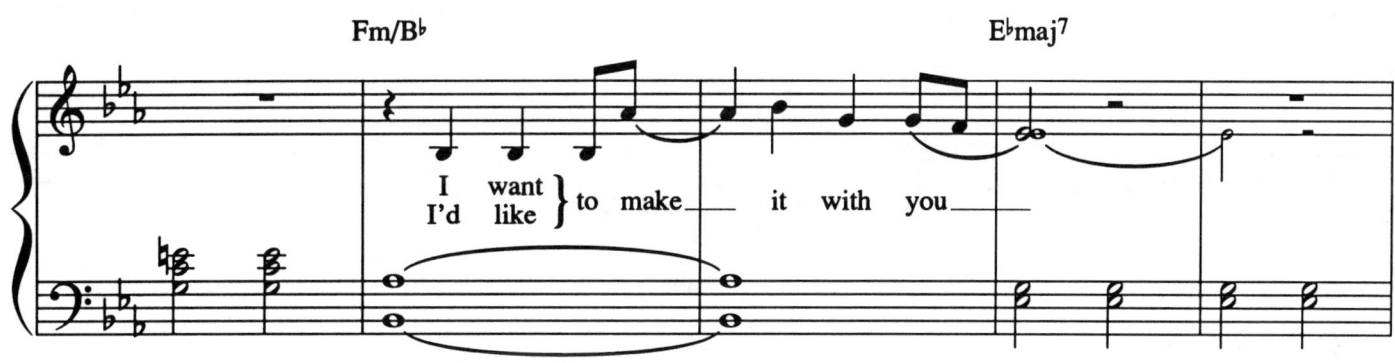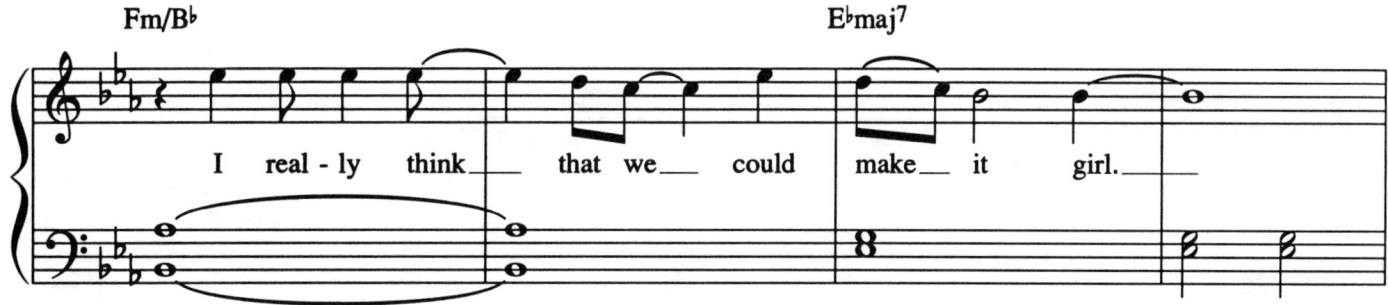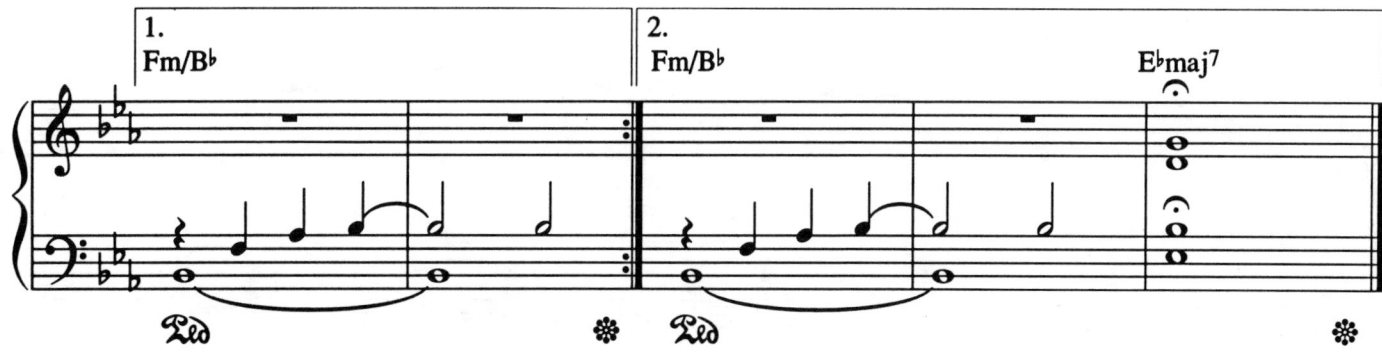

Additional Lyrics

1. I can still recall the wheatfields of Saint Paul,
   And the mornin' we got caught robbin' from an old hen.
   Old MacDonald, he made us work, but then he paid us for what it was worth.
   Another tank of gas and back on the road again.

2. I'll never forget that day we motored stately into big L.A.
   The lights of the city put settlin' down in my brain.
   Though it's only been a month or so, that old car's buggin' us to go.
   You gotta get away and get back on the road again.

Moments to Remember

Lyrics by AL STILLMAN
Music by ROBERT ALLEN

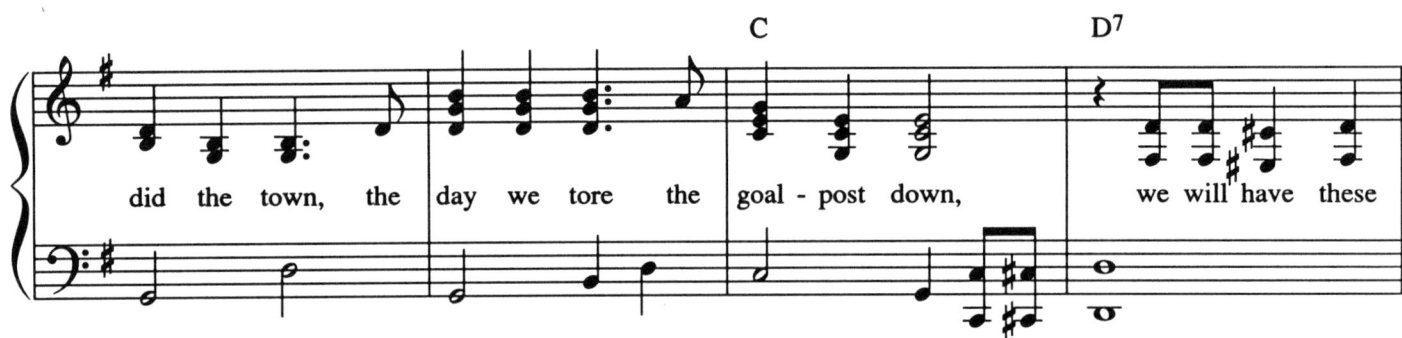
did the town, the day we tore the goal-post down, we will have these

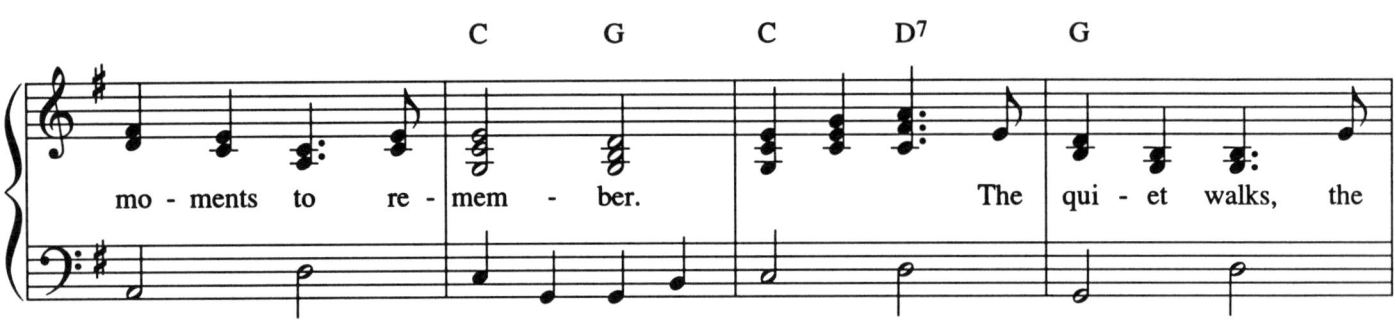
mo - ments to re - mem - ber. The qui - et walks, the

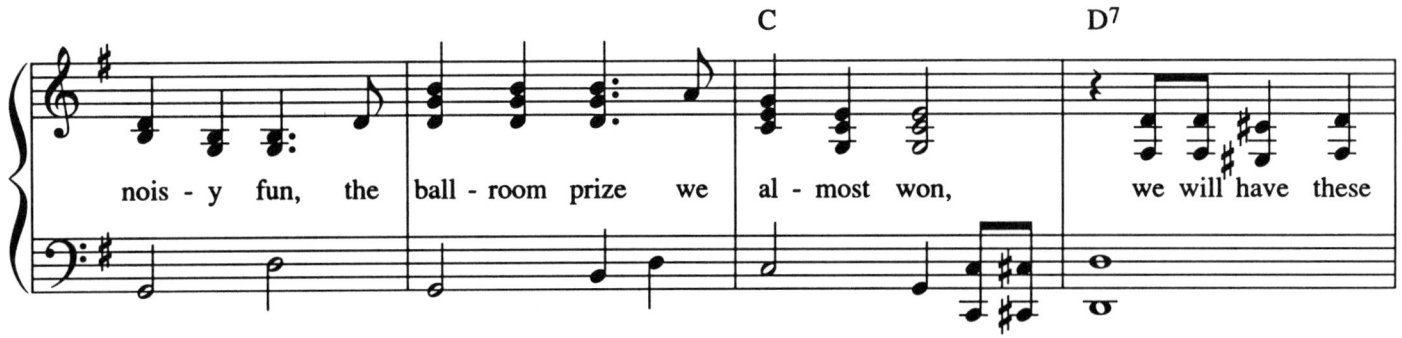
nois - y fun, the ball - room prize we al - most won, we will have these

Copyright © 1955, Renewed 1983 and assigned to Larry Spier, Inc. and Charlie Deitcher Productions, Inc. All rights reserved. International Copyright secured.

My Boy Lollipop

Words and Music by
JOHNNY ROBERTS,
ROBERT SPENCER
and MORRIS LEVY

Oh, Oh, I'm Falling in Love Again

Words and Music by
AL HOFFMAN, DICK MANNING
and MARK MARKWELL

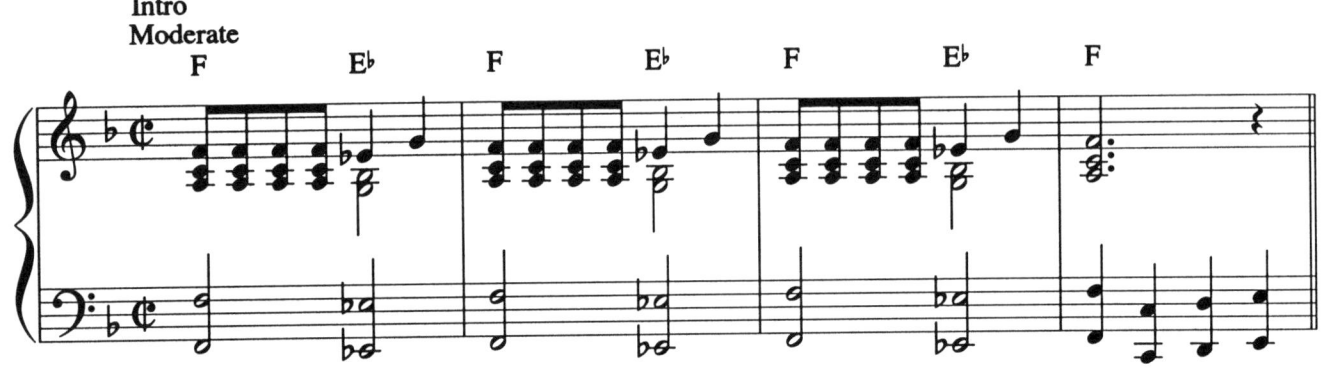

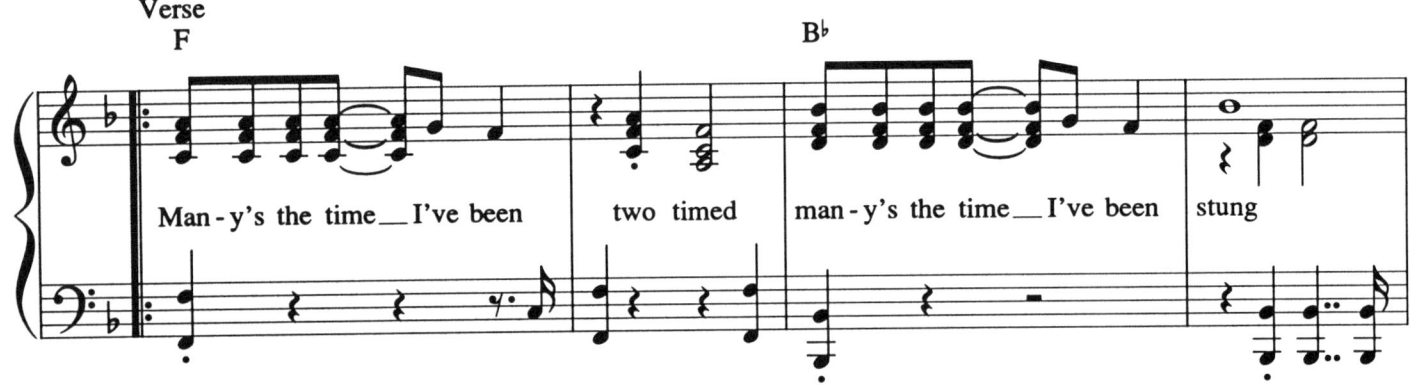
Man-y's the time I've been two timed man-y's the time I've been stung

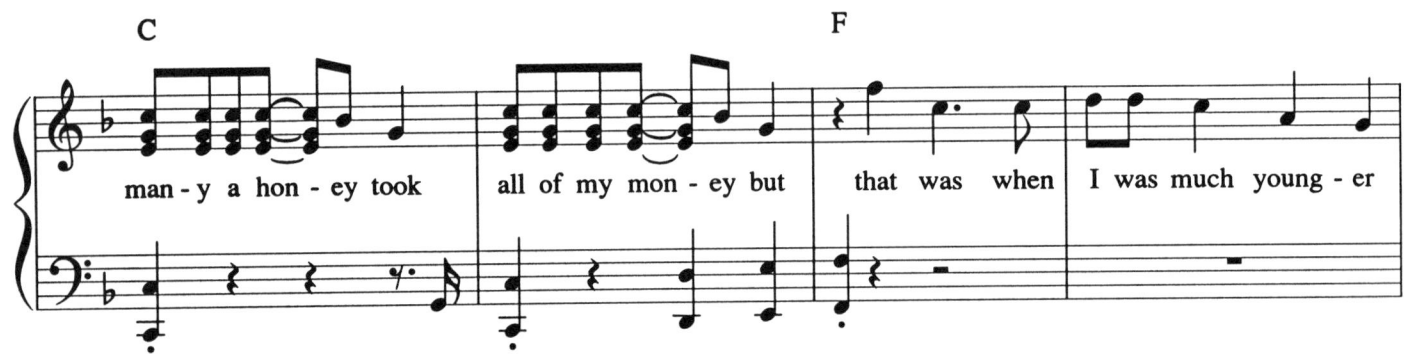
man-y a hon-ey took all of my mon-ey but that was when I was much young-er

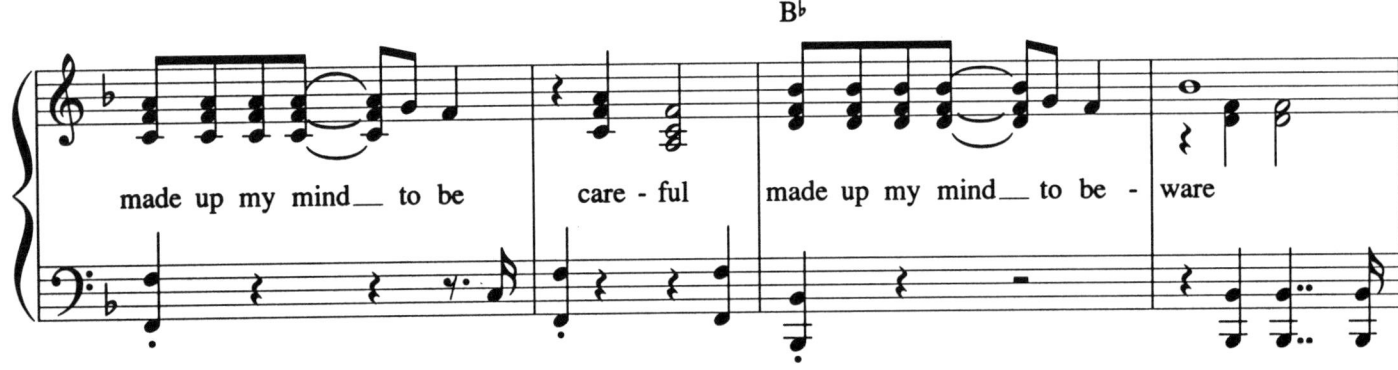
made up my mind to be care-ful made up my mind to be-ware

Oh Carol

Words by HOWARD GREENFIELD
Music by NEIL SEDAKA

Party Doll

Words and Music by
JAMES BOWEN and BUDDY KNOX

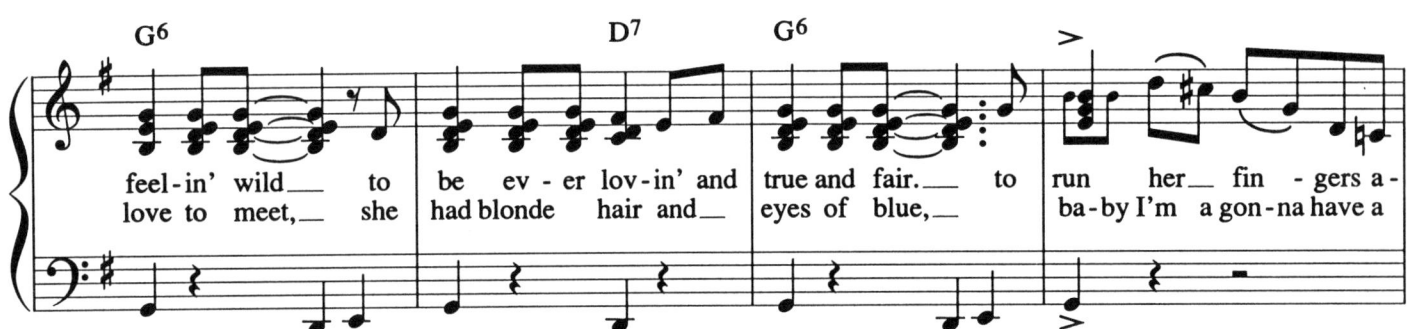

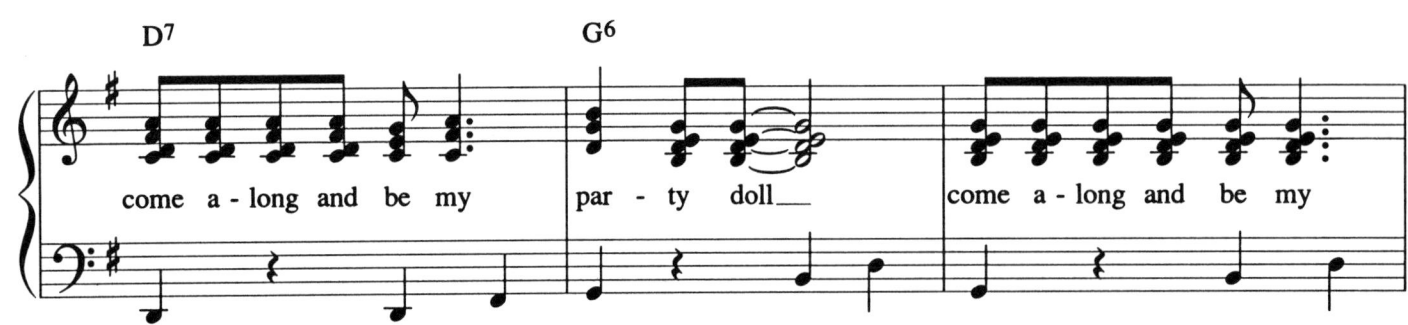

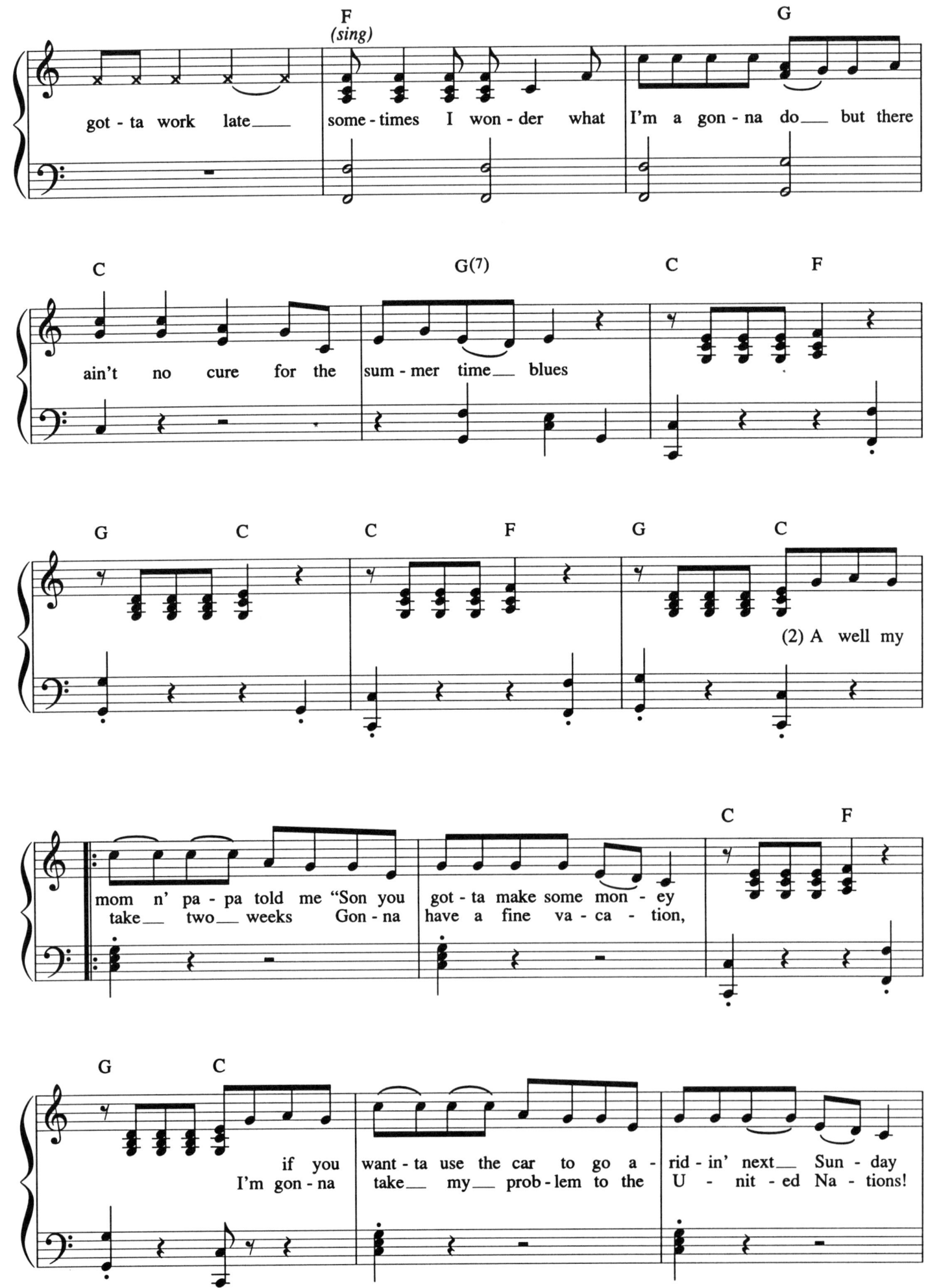

The Rose

Roses Are Red
(My Love)

By AL BYRON and PAUL EVANS

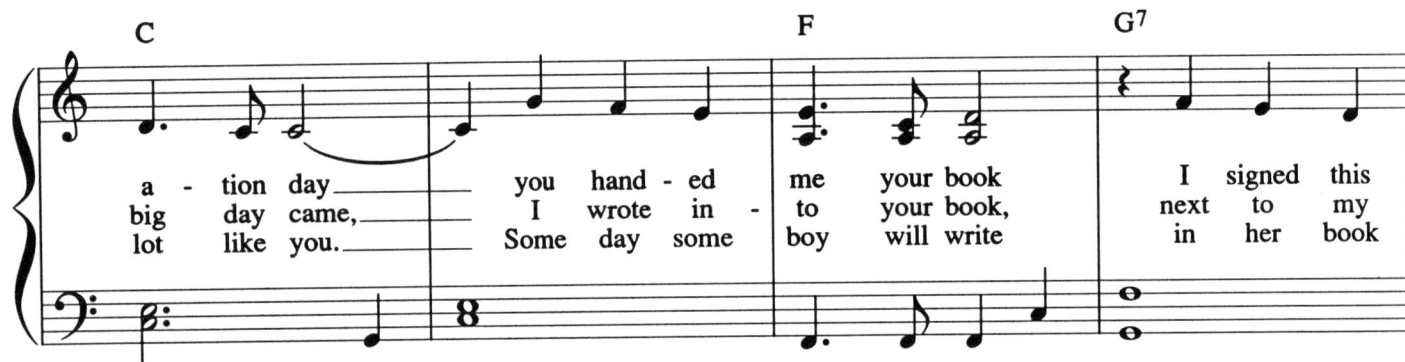

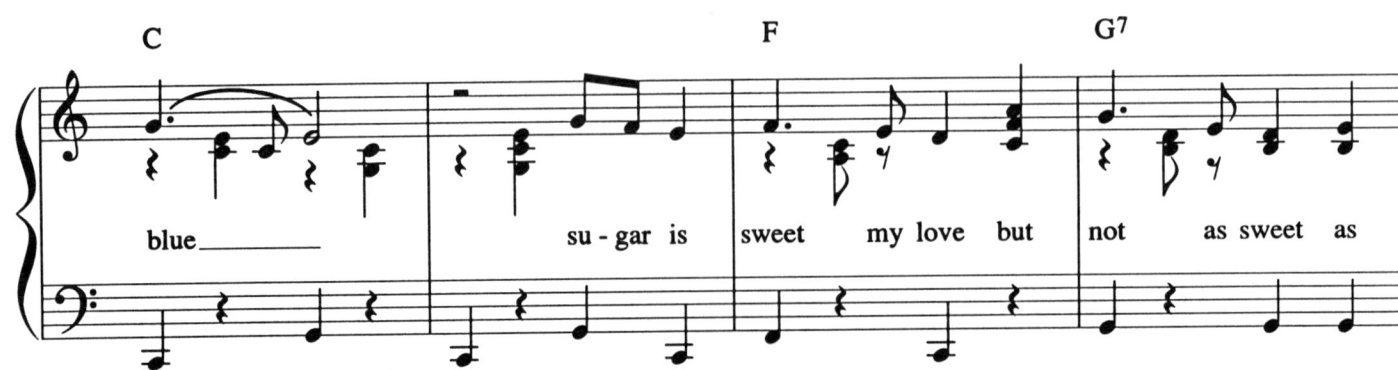

Short Shorts

Words and Music by
THOMAS AUSTIN, BOB GAUDIO,
BILL DALTON and BILL CRANDELL

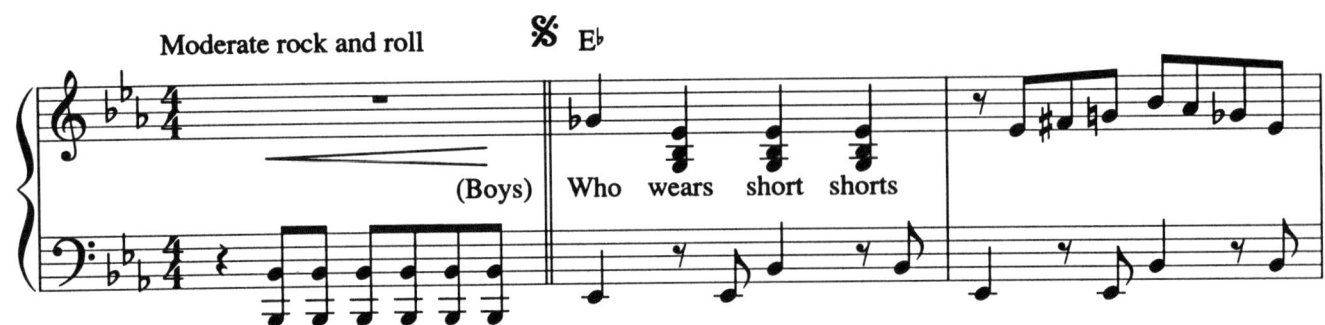

Copyright © 1957 (Renewed) WINDSWEPT PACIFIC ENTERTAINMENT CO. d/b/a LONGITUDE MUSIC CO./NEW SEASONS MUSIC
This arrangement Copyright © 1992 WINDSWEPT PACIFIC ENTERTAINMENT CO. d/b/a LONGITUDE MUSIC CO./NEW SEASONS MUSIC
International Copyright Secured   All Rights Reserved

D.S. and Fade

Theme from A Summer Place

Words by MACK DISCANT
Music by MAX STEINER

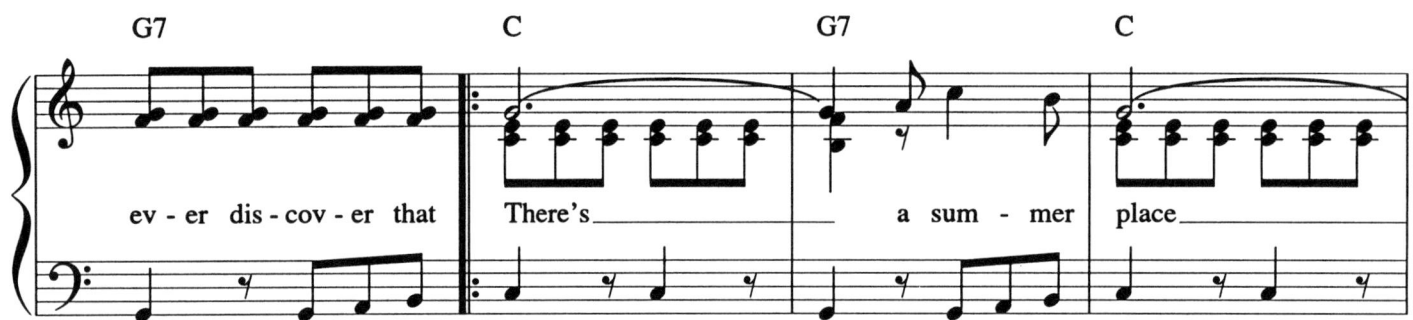
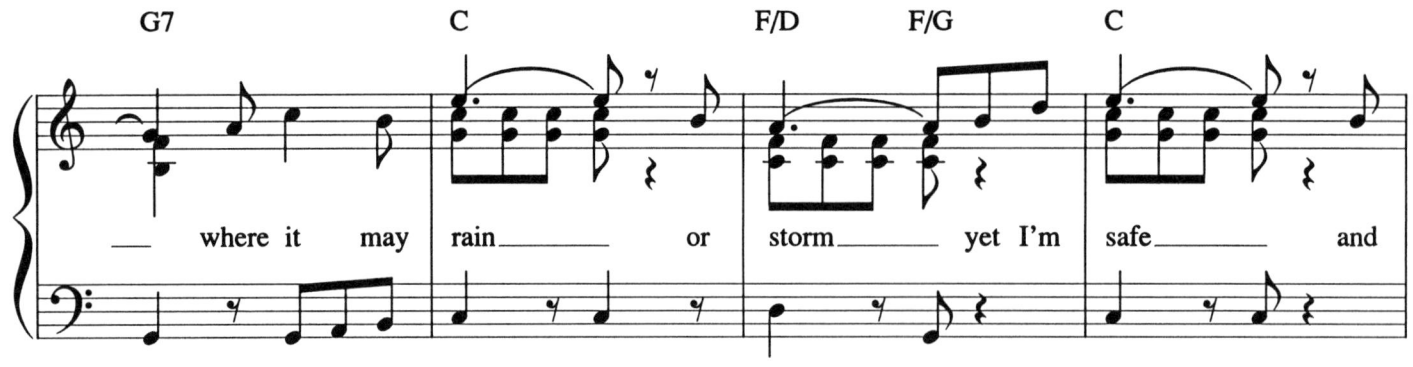
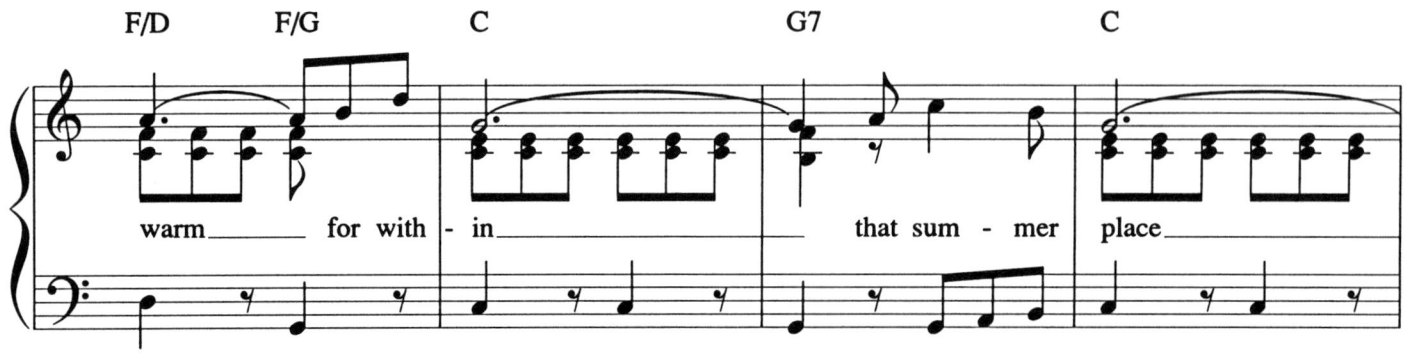

Copyright © 1959, 1960 WARNER BROS. INC.
All Rights Reserved   Used by Permission

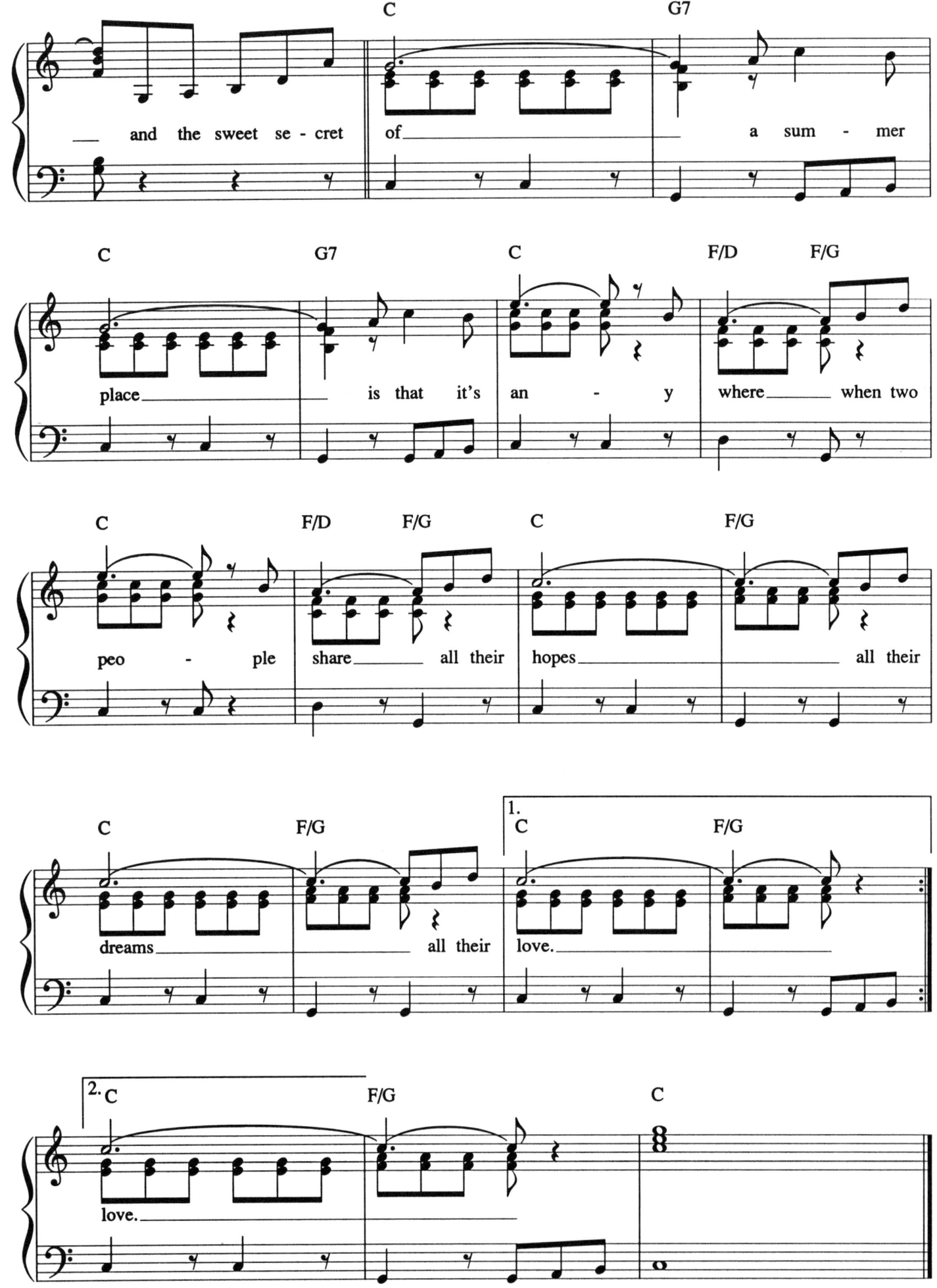

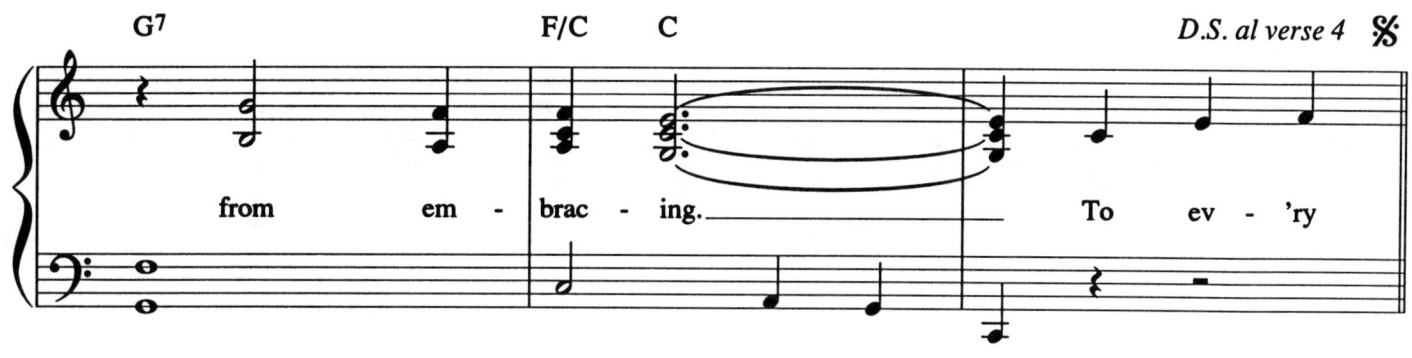

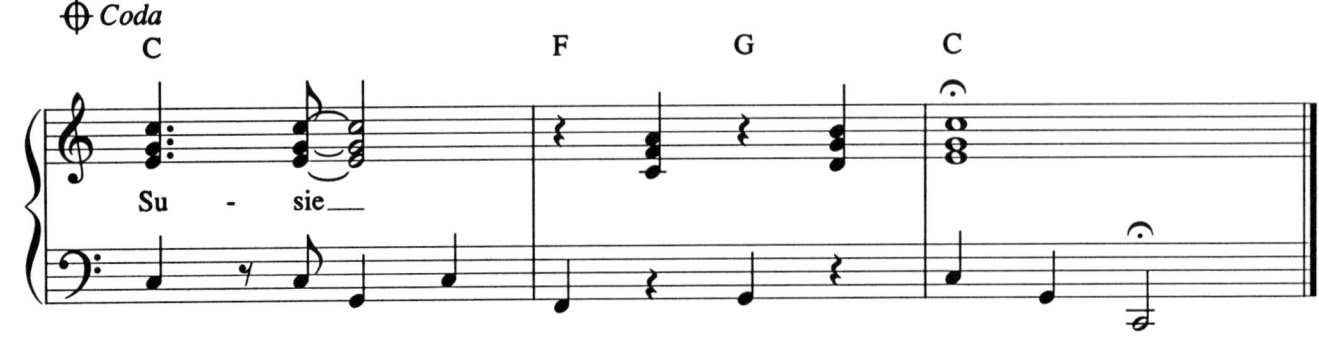

You Belong to the City

Words and Music by
GLENN FREY and JACK TEMPCHIN

Copyright © 1985, 1986 RED CLOUD MUSIC (ASCAP) & NIGHT RIVER PUBLISHING (ASCAP)
All Rights Reserved   Used by Permission

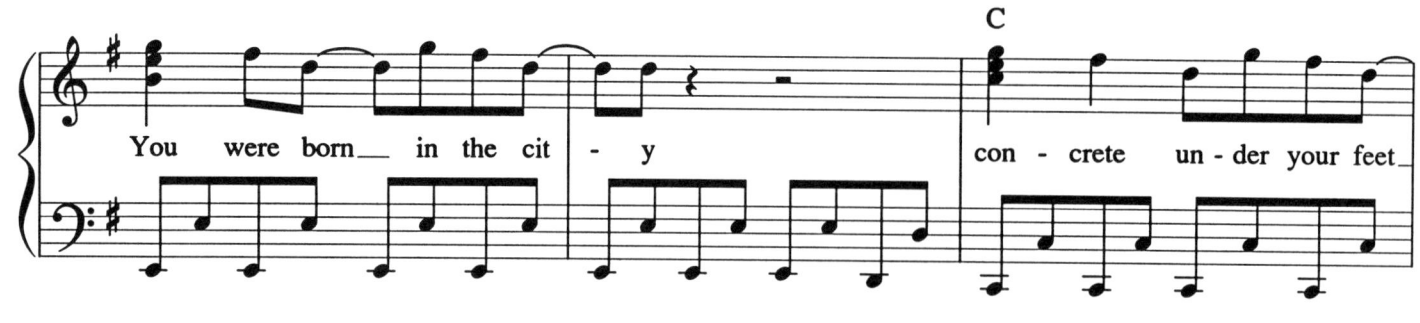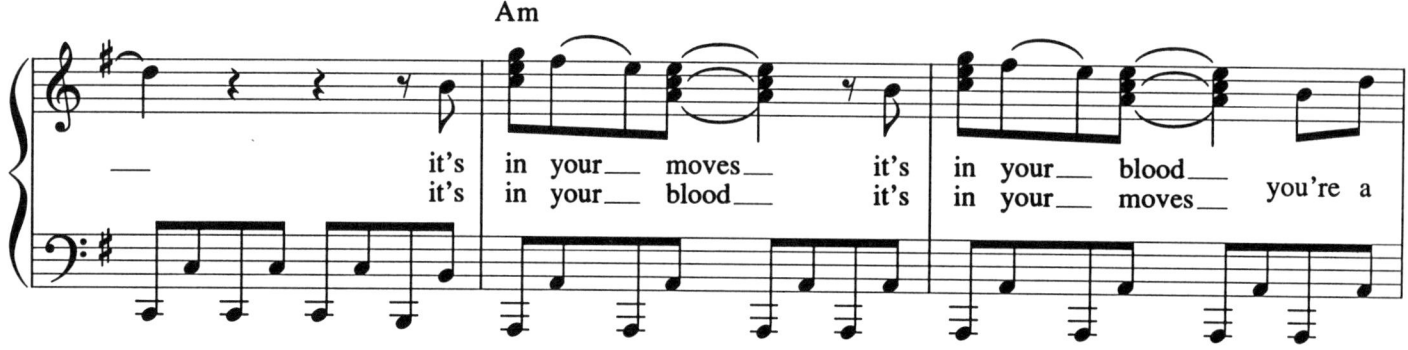